Understanding

EXODUS/ LEVITICUS

Independent of
Earthly Religions

Teresa Yap-Rendon

Understanding

EXODUS

Independent of
Earthly Religions

DEDICATION

I dedicate this book
to every human
who is under bondage,
either a slave to a sinner
or
a slave to sin

TABLE OF CONTENTS

CHAPTER 1

CHAPTER 2

CHAPTER 3

CHAPTER 4

CHAPTER 5

CHAPTER 6

CHAPTER 7

CHAPTER 8

CHAPTER 9

CHAPTER 10

CHAPTER 11

CHAPTER 12

CHAPTER 13

CHAPTER 14

CHAPTER 15

CHAPTER 16

CHAPTER 17

CHAPTER 18

CHAPTER 19

CHAPTER 20

CHAPTER 21

CHAPTER 22

CHAPTER 23

CHAPTER 24

CHAPTER 25

CHAPTER 26

CHAPTER 27

CHAPTER 28

CHAPTER 29

CHAPTER 30

CHAPTER 31

CHAPTER 32

CHAPTER 33

CHAPTER 34

CHAPTER 35

CHAPTER 36

CHAPTER 37

CHAPTER 38

CHAPTER 39

CHAPTER 40

CHAPTER 1

1 Now these are the names of the sons of Jacob (or Israel) who came to Egypt with him, each man with his family, as follows:

[Genesis 46:7; Numbers 20:15a; 1 Chronicles 2:1a; Psalms 105:23; Acts 7:15a]

2 Reuben, Simeon, Levi, Judah,

3 Issachar, Zebulun, Benjamin,

4 Dan, Naphtali, Gad, and Asher

[1 Chronicles 2:1b-2]

5 The total number of persons who descended from Jacob was 70 *(75 in Acts 7:14)*, including Joseph who was already there in Egypt.

[Genesis 46:27b; Deuteronomy 10:22a]

6 Eventually Joseph died, then all his brothers, and that whole generation.

[Acts 7:15b]

7 The Israelites multiplied at an extraordinary rate and spread out in large numbers, and the land was filled with them.

[Genesis 47:27b; Acts 7:17b]

8 Before long a new king, who knew nothing about Joseph, rose to power in Egypt.

[Acts 7:18]

9 And he said to his people: "Look, the Israelites are far more numerous than we are.

[Psalms 105:24]

10 C'mon, let's be smart in dealing with them, lest they become too many, and in the event of war they abandon our country and defect to our enemy."

[Psalms 105:25]

11 So when they embarked on constructing Pithom and Rameses as storage cities for Pharaoh, they set foremen over them to crush them with heavy loads.

12 But the more they oppressed them, the more they multiplied and spread out. As a result, they became allergic to the Israelites.

13 Soon the Egyptians treated the Israelites tyrannically.

[Numbers 20:15b]

14 They made their life miserable with slavish work in mortar and bricks, and in every form of slavery in the construction

field; yes, they treated them tyrannically with every form of slavery.

[Deuteronomy 16:12a; 26:6]

15 Eventually the king of Egypt told the Hebrew midwives, namely, Shiphrah and Puah,

16 saying: "When you assist the Hebrew women giving birth on a stool, kill if it's a boy, but spare if it's a girl."

17 But the midwives feared God, they did not do what the king of Egypt had told them, but let the boys live.

18 Before long the king of Egypt summoned the midwives and asked them: "Why have you let the boys live?"

19 The midwives answered Pharaoh: "Hebrew women are not like Egyptian women, they are energetic. Before a midwife could get to them, they have already given birth."

20 As the Israelites grew in number and became very many, God rewarded the midwives.

21 And because the midwives feared God, He soon gave them families of their own.

[Genesis 42:18; Exodus 14:31a; 20:20; Deuteronomy 4:10; 6:1-2, 13a, 24; 8:6; 31:12; Joshua 4:24; 24:14; 1 Samuel 12:24; 2 Samuel 23:3-4; 1 Kings 8:40, 43; 2 Kings 17:28, 36, 39; 1 Chronicles 16:25; 2 Chronicles 6:31; 19:7; 26:5; Nehemiah 1:11a; 5:9; Job 1:1; 2:3b; 28:28a; 37:24; Psalms 2:11; 5:7b; 15:4a; 19:9a; 25:12, 14; 33:8, 18a; 34:7, 9, 11; 60:4; 61:5b; 66:16; 67:7; 72:5; 85:9; 86:11c; 103:11,

13, 17; 111:5a, 10; 12:1b; 115:11, 13; 118:4; 119:38, 63, 74, 79, 120; 128:1; 145:19; 147:11; Proverbs 1:7a; 2:4-5; 3:7; 8:13a; 9:10a; 10:27a; 14:2a, 26-27; 15:16, 33a; 16:6b; 19:23; 22:4; 23:17-18; 24:21a; 31:30; Ecclesiastes 5:7b; 7:18b; 8:12-13; 12:13; Isaiah 8:13; 11:2-3a; 33:6; 59:19a; Jeremiah 5:22a; 10:7; 26:19; 32:39b; Jonah 1:9b, 16; Micah 6:9; Zephaniah 3:7a; Malachi 1:6b; 3:16; 4:2; Luke 1:50; 12:5; John 9:31; Acts 9:31b; 10:2, 22, 35; 13:26; 2 Corinthians 5:11a; 7:1; Colossians 3:22; Hebrews 5:7; 11:7a; 12:28; 1 Peter 2:17c; Revelation 14:7a; 15:4a; 19:5]

22 Finally Pharaoh commanded all his people, saying: "Throw every *(Hebrew)* newborn baby boy into the Nile River, but spare every baby girl."

[Acts 7:19]

CHAPTER 2

1 Meanwhile, a man of the house of Levi went ahead with marrying a Levite woman.

[Exodus 6:20a; Numbers 26:59a]

2 And the woman became pregnant and gave birth to a son. On seeing how cute he was, she hid him for three months.

[Acts 7:20]

3 When she could no longer hide him, she coated a papyrus basket with asphalt and tar, put the child in it, and placed it among the reeds by the bank of the Nile River.

4 What's more, his sister stood at a distance to see what will happen to him.

5 After a while the daughter of Pharaoh came down to bathe in the Nile River. When her female attendants were strolling by the river, she noticed the basket among the reeds. And at once she sent her maid to get it.

[Acts 7:21a]

6 When she opened it, she saw a baby boy crying.

She felt sorry for him and said: "This is one of those Hebrew babies."

7 At that his sister asked the daughter of Pharaoh: "Shall I go and get a caregiver from the Hebrew women to breastfeed the baby for you?"

8 The daughter of Pharaoh answered her: "Go!"

And right away the girl went and called the baby's mother.

9 The daughter of Pharaoh told her: "Take this baby with you and breastfeed him for me, and I shall pay you."

And the woman took the baby to breastfeed him.

10 When the child was weaned, she brought him to the daughter of Pharaoh, and he became a son to her.

She named him Moses *(meaning 'Drawn out')*, for she said, 'It's because I drew him out of the water.'

[Acts 7:21b]

11 As the years went by, Moses, now a grown up man *(40 years old according to Hebrews 11:23a)*, went to his kinsmen to watch them carry loads. While he was there he saw an Egyptian beating a Hebrew, one of his kinsmen.

[Acts 7:23-24a]

12 When he looked around and saw no one, he killed the Egyptian and hid him in the sand.

[Acts 7:24b]

13 The next day he went out again and this time he saw two Hebrew men fighting.

He asked the aggressor: "Why are you beating your friend?"

[Acts 7:26]

14 He answered: "Who made you ruler and judge over us? Are you going to kill me the way you killed the Egyptian?"

[Acts 7:27-28, 35]

Frightened, Moses said *(to himself)*, 'For sure it has become known!'

15 When Pharaoh heard about it, he attempted to kill Moses, but Moses escaped from his hands and fled to the land of Midian, and there rested by a well.

[Acts 7:29a]

16 Now, as usual, the 7 daughters of the priest of Midian came to draw water to fill the drinking troughs to water their father's flock.

17 And, as usual, the shepherds came and drove them away. At this Moses came to the women's rescue and watered their flock.

18 When they came home, Reuel their father asked: "How come you're home so early today?"

19 They answered: "An Egyptian rescued us from the hands of the shepherds. What's more, he drew water for us and watered the flock."

20 He then asked his daughters: "But where is the man? Why did you leave him behind? Invite him to eat."

21 After that Moses agreed to stay with the man. And the man married off his daughter Zipporah to Moses.

[Exodus 4:25b; 18:2; Numbers 12:1]

22 In time she gave birth to a son, and he named him Gershom *(meaning 'Settler')*, for he said, 'I have become a settler in a foreign land.'

[Exodus 18:3; 1 Chronicles 26:24]

23 Eventually the king of Egypt died. But the Israelites continued to sigh and groan because of the slavish work. And their outcry reached the ears of God.

[Exodus 1:8; 3:7b, 9a; Numbers 20:16; Deuteronomy 26:7a; Nehemiah 9:9a; Acts 7:34]

24 On hearing their groans, God remembered His covenant with Abraham, Isaac, and Jacob.

[Exodus 6:5; Leviticus 26:42, 45; Psalms 106:45]

25 And God turned His face to the Israelites and observed.

CHAPTER 3

1 Moses became a shepherd of the flock of Jehtro *(Reuel in Exodus 2:18 & Numbers 10:29)* the priest of Midian, his father-in-law. While he was tending the flock to the west side of the wilderness, he came by chance to Horeb, the mountain of God.

2 Then the angel of God *drew his attention* to a burning thornbush. And as he looked, he saw the thornbush was on fire but would not burn up.

[Acts 7:30]

3 So Moses said, 'I will go over to check this strange sight, why the thornbush would not burn up.'

[Acts 7:31a]

4 When God saw that he was coming over to check, at once He called him from the midst of the thornbush: "Moses! Moses!"

[Acts 7:31b]

   He answered: "Here I am!"

5 He said: "Do not come any closer. Remove your sandals because the ground on which you are standing is holy."

[Acts 7:33]

6 He went on to say: "I am the God of your forefathers --- the God of Abraham, the God of Isaac, and the God of Jacob."

But Moses hid his face, afraid to look at God.

[Acts 7:32]

7 Jehovah went on: "I have seen the plight of My people who are in Egypt. I have heard their groans because of the of slavish work. I can feel their pain.

[Acts 7:34a]

8 I came down to rescue them from the hand of the Egyptians, to take them out of that land, and to bring them to a good and spacious land, to a land overflowing with milk and honey, to the territory of the Canaanites, Hittites, Amorites, Perizzites, Hivites, and Jebusites.

[Acts 7:34b]

9 When the groans of the Israelites reached My ears, I observed how they are being oppressed by the Egyptians.

[Exodus 2:25; 3:7, 16; Deuteronomy 26:7; Nehemiah 9:9; Acts 7:34a]

10 So now go! I am sending you to Pharaoh to lead My people, the Israelites, out of Egypt."

[Acts 7:34c]

11 But Moses asked God: "Who am I that I should go to Pharaoh and lead the Israelites out of Egypt?"

12 He answered: "I will be with you, and to prove to you that it's I who is sending you, come and worship Me on this mountain after you have led the people out of Egypt."

[Acts 7:7b]

13 Moses asked God: "Suppose I go to the Israelites and say to them , 'The God of your forefathers has sent me to you' --- and they ask me, 'Who is He?' --- What shall I tell them?" ---

14 God answered Moses: *"I will show who I am."*

[Exodus 6:7b; 7:5; 9:16; 10:2; 14:4, 18; 16:2; 29:46; Nehemiah 9:10; Romans 9:17]

He went on: "Say this to the Israelites, 'He, who will show who He is, has sent me to you.'"

15 God went on to say to Moses: "Say this to the Israelites, 'Jehovah *(spelled as 'YHWH' but pronounced as 'EIOUA')*, the God of your forefathers --- the God of Abraham, the God of Isaac, and the God of Jacob --- has sent me to you. That is My name since time immemorial, and that is how I am to be called unto all generations.'

[Exodus 15:3b; Psalms 83:18; 102:12; 135:13; Isaiah 42:8a; Jeremiah 32:18; 33:2; Hosea 12:5; Amos 5:8, 27; 9:6]

16 Go, gather the elders of Israel and say to them, 'Jehovah, the God of your forefathers, the God of Abraham, Isaac, and Jacob, has got in touch with me and said, 'I will by all means pay attention to you and to what is being done to you in Egypt.

[Exodus 3:2, 18a; 4:5; 5:3a]

17 And so I said I will deliver you from the cruelty of the Egyptians and bring you to the land of the Canaanites, Hittites, Amorites, Perizzites, Hivites, and Jebusites, to a land overflowing with milk and honey.'

[Exodus 3:8; Leviticus 20:24; Deuteronomy 7:1; Nehemiah 9:8; Jeremiah 11:5; 32:22; Ezekiel 20:6, 15; Acts 7:34a]

18 If the elders of Israel believe you, then go with them to the king of Egypt and tell him, 'Jehovah, the God of the Hebrews, has got in touch with us. Please allow us to take a 3-day journey into the wilderness and there offer a sacrifice to Jehovah our God.'

[Exodus 3:2, 16a; 4:5; 5:3; 8:27]

19 But I am sure the king of Egypt will not let you go except by a strong hand.

[Exodus 6:1; 13:3a, 9, 14; Deuteronomy 5:15a; 6:21; 7:8; 9:26; 26:8; Psalms 136:11-12; Jeremiah 32:21]

20 So I will have to put out My hand and strike Egypt with all the plagues I am to do in its midst. And afterwards he will let you go.

[Exodus 7:3-4; 12:29, 31; Joshua 24:5]

21 I will also make the Israelites pleasing in the eyes of the Egyptians so that you will not leave empty-handed.

[Exodus 11:3; 12:36a; Deuteronomy 15:13; Psalms 105:37a]

22 Every mother shall ask from her neighbors and from *her friends living near* her house articles of gold and of silver, and clothes for her sons and daughters. Thus you will strip the Egyptians."

[Exodus 11:2; 12:35, 36b; Psalms 105:37a]

CHAPTER 4

1 Moses answered: "Suppose they would not believe me and would not heed my voice, and say, 'Jehovah did not get in touch with you'?"

2 Jehovah asked him: "What is that in your hand?"

He answered: "A rod."

3 He said: "Throw it to the ground."

So Moses threw it to the ground, and it became a serpent, and he fled from it.

4 Jehovah now said to Moses: "Grab it by the tail."

So he grabbed it by the tail, and it became a rod in his hand.

5 He said: "By means of it they will believe that Jehovah, the God of their forefathers, the God of Abraham, the God of Isaac, and the God of Jacob, has got in touch with you.'"

[Exodus 3:2, 16a, 18a; 5:3a]

6 Jehovah went on to say to him: "Please put your hand beneath your garment."

So he put his hand beneath his garment, but when he drew it out, his hand was leprous as white as snow!

7 Then He said: "Put your hand back beneath your garment."

So he put back his hand beneath his garment, and when he drew it out, it was the same as the rest of his skin!

8 He said: "If they will not believe you nor be convinced of the first miracle, for sure they would be convinced of the second.

9 If they will not still believe nor be convinced of these two miracles, then you will have to take some water from the Nile River and pour it on dry land. And the water that you took from the river will become blood, yes, it will become blood on dry land."

[Exodus 7:17]

10 Moses answered Jehovah: "Pardon me, Lord, but I have never been a good speaker, neither in the past nor at this very moment You're speaking with Your servant; I *stutter when I talk.*"

[Exodus 6:12b, 30]

11 Jehovah asked him: "Who made man's mouth, or who makes the mute or the deaf or the seeing or the blind, isn't it I?

[Proverbs 20:12]

12 So go now, and I will be with your mouth; I will dictate to you what you are to say."

[Exodus 4:15]

13 He answered: "Pardon me, Lord, but please send someone else."

14 Disappointed with Moses, Jehovah asked: "How about your brother, Aaron the Levite? I know he can speak well. What's more, he is now on his way to meet you, and he would be happy to see you.

15 Tell him to speak on your behalf, and I will be with your mouth and with his mouth. I will dictate to both of you what you are to say.

[Exodus 4:12]

16 He shall speak to the people on your behalf, serving as your mouth, while you shall serve as god to him.

[Exodus 7:1]

17 And bring this rod with you with which you will do all the plagues."

18 Hence Moses left and returned to Jethro *(Reuel in Exodus 2:18 & Numbers 10:29)*, his father-in-law, and said to him: "Please let me go back to my relatives who are in Egypt to see whether they are still alive."

Jethro answered Moses: "Go in peace."

19 In Midian Jehovah told Moses: "Go back to Egypt, for all the men who were hunting you down are dead."

20 So Moses had his wife and his sons ride on a donkey, and they headed back to Egypt. What's more, Moses brought the rod of God with him.

21 Jehovah went on to say to Moses: "When you're back in Egypt, see to it that you both do the miracles I have empowered you with before Pharaoh. As for Me, I will let him harden his heart, and he will not let the people go.

[Exodus 7:14; 8:32; 9:7b, 35; 10:20, 27; 11:10b]

22 You shall say to Pharaoh, 'This is what Jehovah says, 'Israel is My son, My firstborn.

23 So I'm telling you to let My son *(Israel)* go so that they can worship Me. But in case you refuse to let them go, I am going to kill your son, your firstborn.'"

[Exodus 11:4-5; 12:12a, 29; 13:15a; Psalms 78:51; 105:36; 135:8; 136:10]

24 Now while they were on their way to a lodging place, *God* was morosely contemplating of killing him.

(Note: It was not clear who God was contemplating to kill, if it was Moses or his son who was not circumcised on the 8th day.) [Genesis 17:14]

25 Eventually Zipporah took a sharp stone and circumcised her son, whose foreskin she threw at his feet, saying: "You are a *bloody husband* to me!"

[Exodus 2:21; 18:2]

26 While she was saying, '... *a bloody husband...*' because of the circumcision, He let go of him *(either Moses or his son)*.

27 Jehovah then told Aaron: "Go, meet Moses in the wilderness."

And he met him in the mountain of God and greeted him with a kiss.

28 Moses related to Aaron all the words of Jehovah, the One who sent him, as well as the miracles He told him to do.

[Exodus 4:2-7]

29 Hence Moses and Aaron left and gathered all the elders of Israel.

[Exodus 3:16a]

30 Before the eyes of the elders Aaron spoke all the words that Jehovah has said to Moses, and he performed the miracles.

[Exodus 3:16b]

31 And the people *(elders in Verse 29)* believed. On learning that Jehovah has paid attention to the Israelites and has seen their plight, they bowed down with their faces on the ground.

CHAPTER 5

1 After that Moses and Aaron went to Pharaoh and said: "This is what Jehovah, the God of Israel, says, 'Let My people go so that they can celebrate a feast to Me in the wilderness.'"

[Exodus 3:18b; 5:3b; 8:27]

2 But Pharaoh answered: "Who is Jehovah so that I should heed His voice, to let Israel go? Never heard of Jehovah, and what's more, I'm not going to let Israel go!"

3 They went on to say: "The God of the Hebrews has got in touch with us. Please allow us take a 3-day journey into the wilderness and there offer a sacrifice to Jehovah our God, lest He strike us with pestilence or with sword."

[Exodus 3:2, 16a, 18a; 4:5]

4 The king of Egypt answered them: "Moses and Aaron, why do you want the people to abandon their work? Go, carry your own loads!"

5 Pharaoh went on: "See how many porters there are in the land, and you want them to stop carrying loads?!"

6 So Pharaoh commanded the supervisors and the foremen on that very day, saying:

7 "You shall not supply straw to those who make bricks as before. Let them go and gather straw for themselves.

8 Yet you shall still impose on them the number of bricks that they used to make. Do not reduce one bit for them, they're taking easy. That's why they're saying, 'Allow us to go and offer a sacrifice to our God.' ---

9 Set the quota high on the workers, and let them be busy with it, and don't let them pay attention to nonsense."

10 So their supervisors and foremen went to the workers and said: "This is what Pharaoh says, 'We will not supply straw to you anymore.

11 Get straw yourselves wherever you can find it, yet your quota will not be reduced one bit.'"

12 With that the people scattered all over Egypt to gather stubble *(stalks of grain as substitute)* for straw.

13 And the foremen kept pressuring them, saying: "Meet your daily quota, just as when straw was being supplied."

14 Shortly thereafter the supervisors beat the foremen whom Pharaoh had set over the Israelites, saying: "Why have you not met your quota of bricks as before, both yesterday and today?

15 At that the foremen over the Israelites went in and asked Pharaoh: "Why do you treat your servants this way?

16 There is no straw supplied to your servants, and yet they are telling us to make the same number of bricks! What's more, *we*, your servants, have been beaten up, although it's the fault of your people."

17 He answered: "You're taking easy, you're taking easy! That's why you're saying, 'Allow us to go and offer a sacrifice to Jehovah.'

18 Now get back to work! Although no straw is supplied to you, still you are to make the same number of bricks!"

19 On hearing the words 'Your daily quota of bricks will not be reduced one bit', the foremen over the Israelites saw themselves in a bad situation.

20 After leaving the presence of Pharaoh, they met Moses and Aaron who were waiting for them.

21 Then and there they said to them: "May Jehovah look on you and judge, for you made us stink to Pharaoh and his officials, putting a sword in their hand to kill us."

22 Moses then turned to Jehovah and said: "Lord, why have You caused trouble to this people? Why did You send me?

23 For ever since I went to Pharaoh and spoke in Your name, he has been causing trouble to Your people, yet by no means have you delivered them!"

[Exodus 3:8a]

CHAPTER 6

1 Jehovah answered Moses: "Now you will see what I will do to Pharaoh. By a strong hand, he will let them go; by a strong hand, he will drive them out of his land."

[Exodus 11:1; 12:31-33, 39]

2 God went on to say Moses: "I am Jehovah.

3 I introduced Myself to Abraham, Isaac, and Jacob as God Almighty, but I did not tell them that My name is Jehovah.

4 I also made a covenant with them to give them the land of Canaan, the land where they had lived as settlers.

[Genesis 17:8]

5 When I heard the groans of the Israelites, whom the Egyptians are treating as slaves, I remembered My covenant.

[Exodus 2:24; Leviticus 26:42, 45; Psalms 106:45]

6 So now say to the Israelites, 'I, Jehovah, will take you from under the yoke of the Egyptians, set you free from being their slaves, and redeem you by an Extended Arm and with great plagues.

[Exodus 6:7b; Leviticus 26:13; Deuteronomy 5:15a; 7:8; 15:15; Joshua 24:17a; Jeremiah 2:20a; Ezekiel 34:27b; Micah 6:4]

7 Then I will take you as My people and I will be God to you. Then you shall know who Jehovah your God is that took you out from under the yoke of the Egyptians.

[Deuteronomy 29:13; 2 Samuel 7:24; Jeremiah 7:23; 11:4; 24:7; 30:22; 31:1, 33; 32:38; Ezekiel 11:20; 14:11b; 34:30; 36:28; 37:23c, 27; Hosea 2:23c; Zechariah 8:8b; 13:9c; Romans 9:25-26; 2 Corinthians 6:16c; Hebrews 8:10c]

8 I, Jehovah, will bring you into the land which I promised on oath to Abraham, Isaac, and Jacob that I will give to you as inheritance.'"
9 But when Moses spoke these words to the Israelites, they did not believe him out of frustration and exhaustion.

10 Jehovah then told Moses:

11 "Go to Pharaoh king of Egypt and tell him to allow the Israelites to leave his land."

[Exodus 3:10; 6:26; 1 Samuel 12:6, 8; Acts 7:34c]

12 Moses answered Jehovah: "Look, if the Israelites didn't believe me, why would Pharaoh believe me, for *I stutter when I talk?*"

[Exodus 4:10; 6:30]

13 Still Jehovah gave the command to Moses and Aaron to inform the Israelites and Pharaoh king of Egypt that they are going to lead the Israelites out of Egypt.

[Exodus 6:27]

14 These are the heads of their fathers' houses:

The sons of Reuben, Israel's firstborn, were Hanoch, Pallu, Hezron, and Carmi. This is the family of Reuben.

[Genesis 46:9; Numbers 26:5-7a; 1 Chronicles 5:3]

15 The sons of Simeon were Jemuel, Jamin, Ohad, Jachin, Zohar, and Shaul (the son of a Canaanite woman).

[Genesis 46:10]

(*In Numbers 26:12-13 the sons of Simeon were Nemuel, Jamin, Jachin (Jarib in 1 Chronicles 4:24), Zerah, and Shaul.*)

This is the family of Simeon.

16 The sons of Levi were Gershon, Kohath, and Merari.

[Genesis 46:11; Numbers 3:17; 1 Chronicles 6:1, 16; 23:6]

Levi died at the age of 137.

17 The sons of Gershon were Libni (*Ladan in 1 Chronicles 23:7*) and Shimei.

[Numbers 3:18; 1 Chronicles 6:17]

18 The sons of Kohath were Amram, Izhar, Hebron, and Uzziel.

[Numbers 3:19; 1 Chronicles 6:2, 18; 23:12]

Kohath died at the age of 133.

19 The sons of Merari were Mahli and Mushi.

[Numbers 3:20a; 1 Chronicles 6:19a; 23:21a; 24:26a]

These, then, are the clans of Levi according to their genealogy.

[Numbers 3:20b; 1 Chronicles 6:19b]

20 Amram married Jochebed, his father's sister. In time she bore him Aaron and Moses.

[Exodus 2:1-2; Numbers 26:59; 1 Chronicles 6:3a; 23:13a]

Amram died at the age of 137.

21 The sons of Izhar were Korah, Nepheg, and Zichri.

22 The sons of Uzziel were Mishael, Elzaphan *(Elizaphan in Numbers 3:30)*, and Sithri.

[Leviticus 10:4]

23 Aaron married Elisheba (the daughter of Amminadab and the sister of Nashon). In time she bore him Nadab, Abihu, Eleazar, and Ithamar.

[Numbers 3:2; 26:60; 1 Chronicles 6:3b; 24:1]

24 The sons of Korah were Assir, Elkanah, and Abiasaph *(Ebiasaph in 1 Chronicles 1:23 & 37)*.

This is the family of Korah.

25 Eleazar, Aaron's son, married one of the daughters of Putiel, who in time bore him Phinehas.

[Numbers 25:7a; Judges 20:28a; 1 Chronicles 6:4a]

These, then, are the heads of the fathers' houses of Levi by their clans.

26 This was the Aaron and Moses to whom Jehovah said, 'Lead the Israelites out of Egypt by their army divisions.'

[Exodus 6:11; 7:4; 12:17, 41 51; Numbers 33:1]

27 This was the Moses and Aaron who informed Pharaoh king of Egypt that they are going to lead the Israelites out of Egypt.

[Leviticus 6:13]

28 On that day Jehovah spoke to Moses in Egypt.

29 Jehovah said to Moses: "It's I, Jehovah. Speak to Pharaoh king of Egypt everything that I say to you."

30 Moses answered Jehovah: "Look, *I stutter when I talk,* so why will Pharaoh ever listen to me?"

[Exodus 4:10; 6:12b]

CHAPTER 7

1 Jehovah then told Moses: "Look, I have made you as god to your brother Aaron, and he as your prophet.

[Exodus 4:16]

2 Speak everything that I tell you, and Aaron your brother shall be the one to tell Pharaoh to allow the Israelites to leave his land.

3 As for Me, I will let Pharaoh harden his heart so I can multiply my signs and wonders in Egypt.

[Exodus 10:1; 11:9]

4 If Pharaoh will not listen to you both, then I will have to lay My hand on Egypt and take My army, My people, the Israelites, out of Egypt with great plagues.

[Exodus 6:26; 12:17, 41, 41; Numbers 33:1]

5 When I put out My hand against Egypt and take the Israelites out of their midst, the Egyptians shall know who Jehovah is."

[Exodus 3:14; 6:7b; 9:16; 10:2; 14:4, 18; 16:12; 29:46; Nehemiah 9:10; Romans 9:17]

6 And Moses and Aaron went ahead with doing what Jehovah has told them; they did exactly.

7 Moses was 80 years old and Aaron 83 at the time they spoke to Pharaoh.

8 Jehovah now told Moses and Aaron:

9 "Just in case Pharaoh tells you to do a miracle, tell Aaron to throw down his rod before Pharaoh, and it will become a serpent.'"

[Exodus 4:2-3]

10 And Moses and Aaron went to Pharaoh and did just as Jehovah had told; Aaron threw down his rod before Pharaoh and his officials, and it became a serpent.

11 With that Pharaoh called for the wizards, the witches, and the magicians of Egypt, and they did the same thing by their black magic.

12 Each one threw down his rod, and these became snakes, but the rod of Aaron swallowed their rods.

13 Still the heart of Pharaoh was hard; he did not listen to them, just as Jehovah had foretold.

[Exodus 7:22; 8:15, 19b; 9:12]

14 Jehovah then said to Moses: "Since the heart of Pharaoh is numb, refusing to let the people go, **15** see him in the morning as he goes to the river. Meet him by the riverbank and bring with you the rod which became a serpent.

16 You shall tell him, 'Jehovah, the God of the Hebrews, has sent me to tell you, 'Let my people go so that they can worship Me in the wilderness.'

[Exodus 8:1, 20b; 9:1, 13; 10:3b]

But since you haven't complied until now, **17** this is what Jehovah says, 'By this you shall know who Jehovah is: I am going to strike the water of the Nile River with the rod in my hand, and it will become blood.

18 The fish in the river will die, the river will stink, and the Egyptians cannot stomach to drink its water.'"

19 Then Jehovah told Moses: "Tell Aaron, 'Hold out your rod over the waters of Egypt, over its rivers, over its canals, over its reedy pools, over its impounding reservoirs, and these will become blood. There will be blood everywhere in the land of Egypt, even in stone containers and wood containers."

20 Right away Moses and Aaron did so, just as Jehovah has told. He held out the rod and struck the water of the Nile before the eyes of Pharaoh and of his officials, and all the water of the Nile became blood.

[Psalms 78:44a; 105:29a]

21 The fish that were in the river died, the Nile River stank, and the Egyptians could not stomach to drink its water. Everywhere there was blood in Egypt.

[Psalms 78:44b; 105:29]

22 Nevertheless, the magicians of Egypt did the same thing by their black magic, and the heart of Pharaoh was as hard as ever. He did not listen to them, just as Jehovah had foretold.

[Exodus 7:13; 8:15, 19b; 9:12]

23 Pharaoh, couldn't care less, left and went home.

24 Since the Egyptians could not stomach to drink the water of the Nile, they dug for drinking water around it.

[Exodus 7:18c, 21c]

25 Now seven days have passed since Jehovah had struck the Nile River.

CHAPTER 8

1 Then Jehovah told Moses: "Go to Pharaoh and tell him, 'This is what Jehovah says, 'Let My people go so that they can worship Me.

[Exodus 7:16; 8:20b; 9:1, 13; 10:3b]

2 But if you still refuse to let them go, I am going to infest your entire territory with frogs.

[Psalms 78:45b]

3 The Nile River will swarm with frogs. They will enter your palace and your bedroom, and the homes of your officials and of your people and come up on your couch, in your ovens, and in your kneading troughs.

[Psalms 105:30]

4 Even on you, on your people, and on all your officials the frogs will come up.'"

5 Soon Jehovah told Moses: "Tell Aaron to hold out his rod over the Nile River, over its canals, and over its reedy pools, and frogs will come up on the land of Egypt.'"

6 At once Aaron held out his rod over the waters of Egypt, and frogs came up and covered the land of Egypt.

7 The magicians did the same by their black magic, and frogs came up on the land of Egypt.

8 Soon Pharaoh called for Moses and Aaron and said: "Pray to Jehovah to take the frogs away from me and from my people, for I want now to let the people go so that they can offer a sacrifice to Jehovah."

9 Moses answered Pharaoh: "Have the privilege to say when I will pray for you, for your officials, and for your people, so that the frogs will turn away from you and from your homes, and be limited only in the Nile River."

10 He said: "Tomorrow."

He answered: "Let it be as you say.

For you to know that there is no one like Jehovah God, **11** the frogs will turn away from you, from your officials, from your people, and from your houses, and be limited only in the Nile River."

12 As soon as Moses and Aaron left the presence of Pharaoh, Moses prayed to Jehovah about the frogs He has brought on Pharaoh.

13 And Jehovah heeded the voice of Moses; the frogs died off outside the houses, in the yards, and in the fields.

14 They were piled into heaps, and the land stank.

15 On seeing that there was respite, Pharaoh hardened his heart; he did not listen to them, just as Jehovah had foretold.

[Exodus 7:13, 22b; 8:19b; 9:12]

16 Jehovah then told Moses: "Tell Aaron to hold out his rod and strike the dust of the earth, and these will become *mosquitoes* in all the land of Egypt.'"

17 And they did so. Aaron held out his rod and struck the dust of the earth, and all the dust of the earth became *mosquitoes* in all the land of Egypt, which came on man and on beast.

[Psalms 105:31b]

18 The magicians tried to do the same by their black magic, to produce *mosquitoes*, but they could not. Now the *mosquitoes* came on man and on beast.

19 The magicians said to Pharaoh: "It is the finger of God!"

But the heart of Pharaoh was as hard as ever; he did not listen to them, just as Jehovah had foretold.

[Exodus 7:13, 22b; 8:15; 9:12]

20 Jehovah then told Moses: "Early in the morning meet Pharaoh as he goes to the river. You shall tell him, 'This is what Jehovah says, 'Let My people go so that they can worship Me.

[Exodus 7:16; 8:1; 9:1, 13; 10:3b]

21 But if you're not going to let My people go, I would send flies on you, on your officials, and on your people, and into your houses. And the homes of the Egyptians will be filled with flies, as well as the ground where they are.

[Psalms 105:31a]

22 On that day I will make the land of Goshen distinct, where My people are; no flies will be there so you shall know that I, Jehovah, am in the midst of the land.

[Genesis 47:1; Exodus 9:4, 26; 11:7]

23 Thus I will make a distinction between My people and your people. Tomorrow this sign will happen.'"

24 And Jehovah did it. Dense swarms of flies entered the palace of Pharaoh, the homes of his officials, and all the land of Egypt. As a result, the land was ruined by the flies.

[Psalms 78:45a; 105:31]

25 Finally Pharaoh called for Moses and Aaron and said: "Go, offer a sacrifice to your God within the vicinity."

26 Moses answered: "Is it alright to do so? For what we're going to sacrifice to Jehovah our God is something detestable to the Egyptians. If we were to sacrifice something detestable to the Egyptians in their sight, wouldn't they stone us?

27 Therefore we will take a 3-day journey to the wilderness and there offer a sacrifice to Jehovah our God, just as He has told us."

[Exodus 3:18b; 5:3b]

28 Pharaoh then said: "I will let you go, and you will offer a sacrifice to Jehovah your God in the wilderness; only do not go very far. And pray for me."

[Psalms 99:6a]

29 Moses answered: "As soon as I leave, I will pray to Jehovah, and by tomorrow the flies have already turned away from you, from your officials, and from your people. Only may Pharaoh not play games again by not letting the people go to offer a sacrifice to Jehovah."

30 Then Moses left the presence of Pharaoh and prayed to Jehovah.

31 And Jehovah heeded the voice of Moses; the flies turned away from Pharaoh, from his officials, and from his people. Not one remained.

32 But Pharaoh hardened his heart again; he did not let the people go.

[Exodus 4:21b; 7:14; 9:7b, 35; 10:20, 27; 11:10]

CHAPTER 9

1 Jehovah then told Moses: "Go to Pharaoh and tell him, 'This is what Jehovah, the God of the Hebrews, says, 'Let My people go so that they can worship Me.

[Exodus 7:16; 8:1, 20b; 9:13; 10:3b]

2 But if you still refuse to let them go and you continue to hold them back, **3** the hand of Jehovah would come on your livestock that are out in the field. Your horses, donkeys, camels, herds, and flocks will be afflicted with a severe pestilence.

4 But Jehovah will make a distinction between the livestock of Israel and the livestock of Egypt, not one that belongs to the Israelites will die.

[Exodus 8:22-23; 9:26; 11:7]

5 What's more, Jehovah has scheduled it, saying, 'Tomorrow Jehovah will do it in the land.'"

6 And Jehovah did it the next day; all the livestock of Egypt died, but not one of the livestock of Israel died.

7 Pharaoh sent *(someone to investigate)*, and indeed there was not one dead of Israel's livestock. Yet the heart of Pharaoh was as hard as ever, he did not let the people go.

[Exodus 4:21b; 7:14; 8:32; 9:35; 10:20, 27; 11:10b]

8 Jehovah then told Moses and Aaron: "Take handfuls of ashes, both hands, and Moses will toss them into the air in the sight of Pharaoh.

9 And the ashes will become festering boils breaking out on man and on beast in all the land of Egypt."

10 So they took handfuls of ashes and stood before Pharaoh. Then Moses tossed them into the air, and they became festering boils breaking out on man and on beast.

11 As a result, the magicians could not stand before Moses because of the boils that broke out on them and on all the Egyptians.

12 Jehovah just let Pharaoh harden his heart, and he did not listen to them, just as Jehovah had said to Moses.

[Exodus 7:13, 22b: 8:15, 19b]

13 Jehovah then told Moses: "Early in the morning see Pharaoh, and you shall tell him, 'This is what Jehovah, the God of the Hebrews, says, 'Let My people go so that they can worship Me.

[Exodus 7:16; 8:1, 20b; 9:1; 10:3b]

14 Or this time I am going to make you, your officials, and your people suffer a mortal blow so you shall know that there is no one like Me in the entire earth.

[Exodus 8:10c; 15:11; Deuteronomy 33:26; 1 Samuel 2:2; 2 Samuel 7:22; 1 Kings 8:23; 1 Chronicles 17:20; 2 Chronicles 6:14; Psalms 35:10; 40:5; 71:19; 86:8; 113:5; Isaiah 46:9; Jeremiah 10:6-7; Micah 7:18a]

15 By now I could have put out My hand and afflicted you and your people with pestilence, and you would have been wiped off the face of the earth.

16 But I have kept you alive to show you My power and for the whole world to know who I am.

[Exodus 3:14; 6:7b; 7:5; 10:2; 14:4, 18; 16:12; 29:46; Nehemiah 9:10; Romans 9:17]

17 Since you're still behaving arrogantly against My people, by not letting them go, **18** about this time tomorrow I'm going to send a very heavy hail, the like of which had never happened in Egypt since the day it was founded until now.

19 So now bring into the shelter all your livestock and whatever you have in the field. The hail will fall on every man and beast that are in the open field and not brought into a shelter, and they will die."

20 The officials of Pharaoh who believed the word of Jehovah have their slaves and their livestock brought into shelters.

[Proverbs 22:3a; 27:12a]

21 But those who did not believe the word of Jehovah just left their slaves and their livestock out in the open field.

[Proverbs 22:3b; 27:12b]

22 Jehovah now told Moses: "Raise your hand *(rod in Verse 23)* towards the sky, and hail will fall on all the land of Egypt --- on man, on beast, and on every plant in the fields of Egypt."

23 So Moses raised his rod towards the sky, and Jehovah sent thunder and hail, with lightning striking on the ground. And Jehovah rained hail continuously on the land of Egypt.

[Psalms 105:32]

24 So there was hail, and amidst the hail, there were flashes of lightning. It was the worst, the like of which had never happened before in all the land of Egypt since it became a nation.

25 The hail struck everything that was in the open field throughout Egypt --- man, beast, and plants of every kind. And it shattered all kinds of trees in the fields.

[Psalms 78:47-48; 105:33]

26 Only in Goshen, where the Israelites were, was there no hail.

[Exodus 8:22-23; 9:4; 11:7]

27 Finally Pharaoh called for Moses and Aaron and said to them: "This time I am wrong and Jehovah is right. I and my people have sinned.

28 Pray to Jehovah that this be enough of His thunder and hail. I will let you go, and you shall not stay any longer!"

29 Moses answered him: "As soon as I leave the city, I will pray to Jehovah. The thunder will stop and there will be no more hail. Then you shall know that the earth belongs to Jehovah.

[Psalms 24:1; 50:12b; 1 Corinthians 10:26]

30 But I know that you and your officials do not still fear Jehovah God."

31 (Incidentally, the budding flax and the ripening barley were destroyed, **32** but the wheat and wild grains were not, for they were late crops.)

33 Then Moses left the presence of Pharaoh, and the city, and prayed to Jehovah. And the thunders and the rain stopped, and there was no more hail.

34 On seeing that the rain, the hail, and the thunder stopped, Pharaoh sinned again by hardening his heart, he and his officials.

35 The heart of Pharaoh was as hard as ever; he did not let the Israelites go, just as Jehovah has said to Moses.

[Exodus 4:21b; 7:14; 8:32; 9:7b; 10:20, 27; 11:10b]

CHAPTER 10

1 Jehovah then told Moses: "Go to Pharaoh, for I let him and his officials harden their hearts so I can show My wonders before him.

[Exodus 11:9]

2 This is so that you may relate to your children and grandchildren how severely I dealt with Egypt and what plagues I brought about in their midst, for them to know who Jehovah is."

[Exodus 3:14; 6:7b; 7:5; 9:16; 14:4, 18; 16:12; 29:46; Nehemiah 9:10; Romans 9:17]

3 So Moses and Aaron went to Pharaoh and said to him: "This is what Jehovah, the God of the Hebrews, says, 'How long before you submit yourself to Me? Let My people go so that they can worship Me.

[Exodus 7:16; 8:1, 20b; 9:1, 13]

4 If you still refuse to let My people go, I am going to bring locusts into your territories tomorrow.

5 And they will cover the face of the ground, in that the ground cannot be seen. They will devour what was not destroyed by the hail, that which has been left to you, and they will eat every growth of trees in your fields.

6 Your palace, the homes of all your officials, and the houses in all Egypt will be filled to an extent that your fathers and grandfathers had never seen since the day they existed on earth until now.'"

Then he left Pharaoh.

7 After that the officials of Pharaoh said to him: "How long must this man be a pester to us? Let the men go so that they can worship Jehovah their God! Don't you yet see, Egypt is ruined?"

8 Hence Moses and Aaron were brought back to Pharaoh, and he said to them: "Go, worship Jehovah your God! Who in particular will be going?"

9 Moses answered: "We will go with our young and our old, with our sons and our daughters, and with our sheep and our cattle, for we have a feast to Jehovah."

10 In turn he said to them: "Let it be so, that Jehovah is with you when I let you and your little ones go; for, on the contrary, *I smell something fishy.*

11 No, only the men may go to worship Jehovah, for that is what you've been asking for!"

With that they were driven out from before Pharaoh.

12 Jehovah then told Moses: "Hold out your hand *(rod in Verse 13)* over the land of Egypt, and the locusts will swarm in the land and devour every plant in it, everything that the hail had left."

[Psalms 105:34a]

13 At once Moses held out his rod over the land of Egypt, and Jehovah caused an east wind to blow across the land all day and all night. When the morning came, the east wind has brought the locusts.

14 And the locusts swarmed in the land of Egypt and settled within its boundaries. Never has there been such a dense swarm of locusts nor there will ever be again.

[Psalms 105:34b]

15 They covered the face of the entire land, and the land turned black. And they devoured all the plants in the land and all the fruit of the trees that the hail had left. Nothing green was left on trees or on plants in all the fields of Egypt.

[Psalms 78:46; 105:34-35]

16 Hurriedly, Pharaoh called for Moses and Aaron and said: "I have sinned against Jehovah your God and against you.

[Exodus 9:27a]

17 Please forgive my sin just this once, and pray to Jehovah your God to take this deadly plague away from me."

[Exodus 9:28a]

18 So he left Pharaoh and prayed to Jehovah.

19 And Jehovah turned the *(east)* wind into a very strong west wind, and it carried the locusts into the Red Sea. Not one locust was left in all the territories of Egypt.

[Exodus 10:13]

20 However, Jehovah just let Pharaoh harden his heart, and he did not let the Israelites go.

21 Jehovah then told Moses: "Raise your hand towards the sky, and there will be darkness over the land of Egypt, a darkness that can be felt."

22 Right away Moses raised his hand towards the sky, and a gloomy darkness occurred over the land of Egypt 3 days.

[Psalms 105:28a]

23 For 3 days they did not see one another and no one of them left his house. On the other hand, there was light in all the houses of the Israelites.

24 After that Pharaoh called for Moses and said: "Go, worship Jehovah! Your little ones may go with you, but leave behind your sheep and your cattle."

25 Moses answered: "Give us animal sacrifices and burnt offerings as well, which we shall present to Jehovah our God.

26 Our livestock will go with us, not a hoof will be left behind, for we will choose from them which to sacrifice to Jehovah our God. For we don't know yet which to sacrifice to Jehovah until we get there."

27 Jehovah just let Pharaoh harden his heart, and he did not let them go.

[Exodus 4:21b; 7:14; 8:32; 9:7b, 35; 10:20; 11:10b]

28 Pharaoh told him: "Get away from me! Beware, don't try to see my face again, for on the day you see my face you shall die!"

29 Moses answered: "As you say, I will not try to see your face again!"

CHAPTER 11

1 Jehovah now said to Moses: "I am going to bring one more plague on Pharaoh and on Egypt, and after that he will let you go. And not only will he let you go, he will drive you out altogether from here!

[Exodus 6:1; 12:31-33, 39]

2 So now tell everyone, man or woman, to ask from their friends articles of gold and articles of silver."

[Exodus 3:22; 12:35; Psalms 105:37a]

3 Hence Jehovah made the people pleasing in the eyes of the Egyptians. In fact, the man Moses was very great in Egypt in the eyes of Pharaoh's officials and in the eyes of the people.

[Exodus 3:21; 12:36]

4 And Moses said: "This is what Jehovah says, 'About midnight I will go out in the midst of Egypt, **5** and every firstborn in Egypt must die, from the firstborn of Pharaoh sitting on the throne to the firstborn of the maidservant grinding grain, as well as every firstling of beast.

[Exodus 4:23; 12:12a, 29; 13:15a; Psalms 78:51; 105:36; 135:8; 136:10]

6 And there will be loud cries in all the land of Egypt, the like of which has never happened nor will ever happen again.

[Exodus 12:30]

7 Yet not a dog will bark against any Israelite, from man to beast, for you all to know that Jehovah can man a distinction between Egyptians and Israelites.

[Exodus 8:22-23; 9:4, 26]

8 All these officials of yours will come to me, bow down to me, and say, 'Go, you and all your followers!' --- And after that we will go!"

[Exodus 12:32]

   Seething with anger, he left Pharaoh.

9 Jehovah then said to Moses: "Pharaoh will not listen to you so I can multiply My wonders in the land of Egypt."

[Exodus 10:1]

10 Although Moses and Aaron have done all the plagues before Pharaoh, Pharaoh did not allow the Israelites to leave his land; Jehovah just let him harden his heart.

[Exodus 4:21b; 7:14; 8:32; 9:7b, 35; 10:20, 27]

CHAPTER 12

1 In Egypt Jehovah said to Moses and Aaron:

2 "This month *(Abib in Exodus 13:4 and Nisan in Esther 3:7)* is to be your first month. It will be the 1st month of the year for you.

3 Tell the whole Israelite community, 'On the 10th day of this month, everyone shall bring a lamb to his father's house; one lamb per house.

[Exodus 12:21]

4 But if the household is too small for the lamb, he and his nearest neighbor should share it. They shall divide the lamb among the number of persons and apportion it according to each one's appetite.

5 The lamb should be without defect, male, a year old. It could be a lamb or a kid goat.

[Leviticus 12:21; 22:19-20; Deuteronomy 15:21; 17:1; Malachi 1:13-14; 1 Corinthians 5:7b; 1 Peter 1:18-19]

6 Keep it until the 14th day of this month, the day the whole Israelite community shall slaughter it between sunset and dusk.

[Leviticus 23:5; Numbers 9:2-5; 28:16; Deuteronomy 16:6; Joshua 5:10; 2 Chronicles 30:15a; 35:1; Ezra 6:19; Ezekiel 45:21a]

7 They shall spatter some of the blood on the 2 doorposts and on the lintel above the door of the house where you will eat it.

[Exodus 12:22a; Hebrews 11:28a]

8 That very night they shall roast it with fire and eat it along with unleavened bread and bitter herbs.

[Exodus 23:18a; 34:25a; Numbers 9:11b]

9 Do not eat any part of it half-done. You may boil it with water and then roast it with fire, along with its head, legs, and entrails.

[Leviticus 1:13; 8:21]

10 You shall not leave any of it till morning. Whatever is left till morning you shall burn up.

[Exodus 23:18b; 29:34; 34:25b; Leviticus 7:15; 8:32; 19:6b; 22:30b; Numbers 9:12a; Deuteronomy 16:4b]

11 This is how you shall eat it: Eat it with belt on your waist, sandals on your feet, and walking cane in your hand. And you shall eat it in haste, it is the Passover of Jehovah.

[Exodus 12:39]

12 I, Jehovah, will enter Egypt that night and kill every firstborn in Egypt, from man to beast, punishing all the god-*kings* of Egypt.

[Exodus 4:23; 11:4-5; 12:29; 13:15a; Psalms 78:51; 105:36; 135:8; 136:10]

13 The blood on the house will indicate that you are there. When I see the blood, I will pass over you when I strike the land of Egypt, and the *Destroyer* will not come to you.

[Exodus 12:23, 27; Hebrews 11:28b]

14 You shall commemorate this day; celebrate it as a feast of God throughout your generations. Celebrate it, that is a lasting ordinance!

[Exodus 12:24-27, 47-48; Deuteronomy 16:1; 2 Chronicles 35:17; Ezekiel 45:21a; Luke 22:1]

15 Eat unleavened bread 7 days. On the 1st day remove any yeast from your house. The person who eats anything with yeast during the 7-day period shall be purged from Israel.

[Exodus 12:19-20; 13:6a, 7; Deuteronomy 16:3-4a; 1 Corinthians 5:7a]

16 The 1st day is a holy day, as well as the 7th day. Do no hard work on such days. Only what a person needs to eat, that alone may be done.

[Leviticus 23:7a, 8b]

17 You shall commemorate the Feast of Unleavened Bread, the day I will take your armies out of Egypt. Commemorate this day throughout your generations, it is a lasting ordinance.

[Exodus 23:15; 34:18; Leviticus 23:6a; Deuteronomy 16:16; 2 Chronicles 8:13; 30:21; 35:17; Ezra 6:22a; Ezekiel 45:21b; Luke 22:1; Acts 12:3b; 1 Corinthians 5:8]

18 Eat unleavened bread from the evening of the 14th day *(15th day in Leviticus 23:6)* to the evening of the 21st day on the 1st month.

[Exodus 12:18; 23:15b; 34:18b; Leviticus 23:6; Numbers 28:17]

19 These 7 days no yeast is to be found in your houses. The person who eats anything made with yeast, whether he is a settler or a citizen of the land, shall be purged from the Israelite community.

[Exodus 12:15b; 13:7b; Deuteronomy 16:4a; 1 Corinthians 5:7a]

20 Eat nothing made with yeast; eat unleavened bread wherever you are.'"

21 At once Moses called for all the elders of Israel and told them: "Select a lamb or a kid goat in proportion to the size of your family and slaughter it as Passover sacrifice.

[Exodus 12:3-5; Leviticus 12:5]

22 You shall put its blood in a basin, dip a bunch of hyssop in it, and spatter some of the blood on the lintel above your door and on your 2 doorposts. And no one of you shall leave his house till morning.

[Exodus 12:7; Hebrews 11:28a]

23 When Jehovah passes by to punish the Egyptians and sees the blood on the lintel above your door and on your 2 doorposts, He will pass over your door and not let the Destroyer enter your house to punish you.

[Exodus 12:13, 27; Hebrews 11:28b]

24 Commemorate it, you and your children, that's a lasting ordinance.

[Exodus 12:14, 25-27, 47-48; Deuteronomy 16:1; 2 Chronicles 35:17; Ezekiel 45:21a; Luke 22:1]

25 And when you are in the land that Jehovah will give you, just as He has declared, you shall observe this occasion.

[Exodus 13:5]

26 In case your children ask you, 'What is the essence of this occasion to you?' ---

[Exodus 13:8]

27 this shall be your answer, 'Jehovah passed over our house; He passed over the houses of the Israelites in Egypt when He punished the Egyptians.'"

[Exodus 12:13, 23; Hebrews 11:28b]

With that the people bowed down with their faces on the ground.

28 And the Israelites went and did so, just as Jehovah has told Moses and Aaron; they did exactly.

29 Midnight came, and Jehovah killed all the firstborns in Egypt, from the firstborn of Pharaoh sitting on the throne to the firstborn of the prisoner in the dungeon, as well as every firstling of beast.

[Exodus 4:23; 11:4-5; 12:12a; 13:15a; Psalms 78:51; 105:36; 135:8; 136:10]

30 In the middle of the night Pharaoh got up, as well as all his officials and all the Egyptians. And there were loud cries among the Egyptians for there was not a house where there was not one dead.

[Exodus 11:6]

31 That very night he called for Moses and Aaron and said: "Get up, get away from my people, you and the Israelites! Go, worship Jehovah, just as you've said!

[Exodus 6:1; 11:1; 12:39]

32 Take your flocks and your herds, just as you've said, and leave! But bless me first."

33 Even the Egyptians urged the people to leave the land immediately, saying, 'We are all as good as dead!'

[Deuteronomy 16:3; Psalms 105:38]

34 Thus the people took their flour from their kneading troughs, before yeast was added, and carried them on their shoulders.

[Exodus 12:39]

35 And the Israelites did what Moses told them; they went and asked from the Egyptians articles of gold and of silver, as well as clothes.

[Exodus 3:22a; 11:2; Psalms 105:37a]

36 And because Jehovah made the people pleasing in the eyes of the Egyptians, they gave them what they asked for. Thus they stripped the Egyptians.

[Exodus 3:21, 22b; 11:3]

37 Then the Israelites, about 600,000 able men, aside from *(the women and)* the little ones, left Rameses for Succoth.

[Numbers 11:21; 33:3a, 5]

38 A mixed multitude went with them, along with flocks and herds, a very large number of livestock.

39 Then they made the flour, that which they have taken from Egypt, into loaves of unleavened bread. These were made without yeast because they were compelled to leave Egypt hastily, having had no time to prepare any food for themselves.

[Exodus 12:31-34; Deuteronomy 16:3b]

40 The total number of years the Israelites lived as settlers in Egypt was 430.

[Genesis 15:13; Acts 7:6; Galatians 3:17]

41 At the end of the 430 years, on this very day, the whole army of Jehovah went out of Egypt.

[Exodus 6:26; 7:4; 12:17, 51; Numbers 33:1]

42 And because Jehovah took them out of Egypt that night, it is a night to be remembered by the Israelites throughout their generations.

[Exodus 13:10]

43 Jehovah went on to say to Moses and Aaron: "These are the regulations for the Passover:

No *non-Israelite* may eat of it.

44 If there are slaves bought with money, you shall circumcise them first before they may partake of it.

[Genesis 17:13]

45 Settlers or hired workers may not eat of it.

[Leviticus 22:10b]

46 It is to be eaten in one house. You may not bring any of its meat from one house to another. You shall not break any of its bones.

[Numbers 9:12b; Psalms 34:20; John 19:33, 36]

47 The whole Israelite community is to celebrate it.

[Exodus 12:14, 24-27; Deuteronomy 16:1; 2 Chronicles 35:17; Ezekiel 45:21a; Luke 22:1]

48 In case a settler in your midst wishes to celebrate the Passover of Jehovah with you, let every male of his be circumcised first before he can come to celebrate it like a citizen of the land. For no uncircumcised man may eat of it.

49 One law applies to the citizens and settlers in your midst."

[Numbers 9:14; 15:16]

50 And all the Israelites did so, just as Jehovah had told Moses and Aaron; they did exactly.

51 Thus that very day Jehovah took the Israelites out of Egypt by their army divisions.

[Exodus 6:26; 7:4; 12:17, 41; Numbers 33:1]

CHAPTER 13

1 Jehovah went on to say to Moses:

2 "Dedicate to Me every firstborn male that opens the womb among the Israelites, of man and of beast. They are Mine.

[Genesis 4:4; Exodus 13:12; 22:29b; 34:19; Numbers 18:15a; Deuteronomy 15:19; Luke 2:23]

3 And Moses told the people: "Commemorate the day you came out of Egypt, from the land of slavery, for by a strong hand Jehovah took you out of here. Hence nothing made with yeast may be eaten.

4 This day of the month of Abib *(Nisan in Esther 3:7)* you are leaving.

[Exodus 23:15b; 34:18b; Deuteronomy 16:1]

5 When Jehovah brings you into the land of the Canaanites, Hittites, Amorites, Hivites, and Jebusites, which He promised on oath to your forefathers to give to you, a land overflowing with milk and honey, observe this occasion on such date.

[Exodus 13:4]

6 Eat unleavened bread 7 days, and the 7th day is a feast to Jehovah.

[Exodus 12:15-16, 18, 20; 13:3b, 6-7a; 23:15b; 34:18b; Leviticus 23:6b, 8; Numbers 28:17b; Deuteronomy 16:3, 8]

7 Aside from eating unleavened bread 7 days, nothing with yeast or any sourdough is to be seen within your territory.

[Exodus 12:15, 19; 13:7b; Deuteronomy 16:4a; 1 Corinthians 5:7a]

8 You shall say to your children on that day, 'It's because of what Jehovah has done for me, He took us out of Egypt.'

[Exodus 20:2]

9 It must serve as a bracelet on your wrist and as a frontlet between your eyes, that the Law of Jehovah may be in your mouth, for by a strong hand Jehovah took you out of Egypt.

[Exodus 13:16; Deuteronomy 6:8; 11:18]

10 You shall celebrate its anniversary every year.

[Exodus 12:42]

11 When Jehovah brings you into the land of the Canaanites, just as He has promised on oath to your forefathers to give to you, **12** you shall dedicate to Jehovah every male that opens the womb, and every firstling of beast that belongs to you.

[Genesis 4:4; Exodus 13:2; 22:29b; 34:19; Numbers 18:15a; Deuteronomy 15:19; Luke 2:23]

13 Redeem every firstling of a donkey with a sheep. If you will not, you should break its neck. More so, redeem every firstborn son of man among you.

[Exodus 13:15b; 34:20a; Numbers 18:15b]

14 In case your son asks you in the future, saying, 'What is the essence of this?' --- you shall answer him, 'By a strong hand Jehovah took us out of Egypt, from the land of slavery.

[Exodus 3:19; 6:1; 13:3a, 9; Deuteronomy 5:15a; 6:21; 7:8; 9:26; 26:8; Psalms 136:11-12; Jeremiah 32:21]

15 When Pharaoh stubbornly refused to let us go, God killed every firstborn in Egypt, from the firstborn of man to the firstling of beast. That is why I am dedicating to Jehovah every male that opens the womb, and why I redeem every firstborn son among us.

[Exodus 4:23; 11:4-5; 12:12a, 29; Psalms 78:51; 105:36; 135:8; 136:10]

16 It must serve as a bracelet on your wrist and as a frontlet between your eyes, that by a strong hand Jehovah took us out of Egypt.

[Exodus 13:9; Deuteronomy. 6:8; 11:18]

17 When Pharaoh let the people go eventually, God did not lead them via Philistia, although it was shorter, for God said, 'Lest the people think of returning to Egypt when they see war.'

18 Thus God made the Israelites marched out of Egypt in battle formation and made them go around via the wilderness by the Red Sea.

[Psalms 136:16; Ezekiel 20:10]

19 Moses brought with him the bones of Joseph, who made Israel's sons solemnly swear, saying, 'When God turned His face to you, you must take my bones out of here and bring them with you.'"

[Genesis 50:25; Joshua 24:32; Hebrews 11:22]

20 And they left Succoth and encamped in Etham, on the edge of the wilderness.

[Numbers 33:6]

21 Jehovah led them in a pillar of cloud by day to guide them on the way, and in a pillar of fire by night to give them light.

[Exodus 14:20; 40:38; Numbers 9:16; 14:14c; Deuteronomy 1:33; Nehemiah 9:12, 19; Psalms 78:14; 105:39; Isaiah 4:5]

22 And the pillar of cloud by day, and the pillar of fire by night, would not move away from before the people.

CHAPTER 14

1 Now God told Moses:

2 "Tell the Israelites to turn back and encamp in Pi-Hahiroth, between Migdol and the *(Red)* sea, overlooking Baal-Zephon.

[Exodus 14:9; Numbers 33:7]

3 Thus Pharaoh will be led to think, saying, 'The Israelites have lost their way, they were trapped in the wilderness.'

4 I will just let Pharaoh harden his heart, and he will surely chase after you. When I get glory over Pharaoh and his entire army, the Egyptians shall know who Jehovah is."

[Exodus 3:14; 6:7b; 7:5; 9:16; 10:2; 14:18; 16:2; 29:46; Nehemiah 9:10; Romans 9:17]

And they did exactly.

5 As soon as it was reported to Pharaoh king of Egypt that the people have fled, he and his officials regretted letting the people go, saying, 'What have we done, we have let the Israelites go free from being our slaves?'

6 So he had his war chariots ready and took his troops with him.

7 He took the best 600 chariots, along with all the other chariots of Egypt, with chariot-warriors on each one of them.

8 God just let Pharaoh king of Egypt harden his heart, and he chased after the Israelites who have left with raised fists.

[Numbers 33:3b; Acts 13:17]

9 The Egyptians chased after them with all of Pharaoh's war horses, chariot-warriors, and army, and they caught up with them while they were encamped in Pi-Hahiroth by the sea, overlooking Baal-Zephon.

[Joshua 24:6]

10 On seeing Pharaoh getting close by and the Egyptians marching towards them, the Israelites cried out to Jehovah in fear.

[Joshua 24:7a; Nehemiah 9:9b]

11 And they blamed Moses: "Is it because there is no graveyard in Egypt so that you've brought us here, to die in the wilderness? What have you done to us, leading us out of Egypt?!

12 Didn't we tell you while in Egypt, 'Leave us alone serving the Egyptians!' --- For it's better for us to be serving the Egyptians than to die in the wilderness!"

13 Moses answered the people: "Do not be afraid. Stand still and see the salvation of Jehovah, which He will do for you today. The Egyptians whom you see today, you will not see anymore, no, never again!

[Exodus 14:30; Deuteronomy 1:29; 3:22a; 20:3; 2 Chronicles 20:15a, 17; Jeremiah 1:8, 19]

14 Jehovah will be the one to fight for you, just be still!"

[Exodus 14:25; Deuteronomy 1:30; 3:22b; 20:4; Joshua 10:14, 42; 23:10; 2 Chronicles 20:15b]

15 Jehovah now said to Moses: "Why are you crying out to Me? Tell the Israelites to break camp!

16 As for you, hold out your hand over the sea, and it will split apart, so that the Israelites can walk across the sea on dry ground.

17 As for Me, I will let the Egyptians harden their hearts, and they will chase after you.

After I get glory over Pharaoh and his army, his war horses, and his chariot-warriors, **18** the Egyptians shall know who Jehovah is."

[Exodus 3:14; 6:7b; 7:5; 9:16; 10:2; 14:4, 8-9; 16:12; 29:46; Nehemiah 9:10; Romans 9:17]

19 Now the angel of God who was leading the camp of Israel went behind them.

[Genesis 48:16a; Exodus 3:2; 23:20-23; 32:34b; 33:2; Isaiah 63:9b; Acts 7:30, 35b]

Likewise, the pillar of cloud left their caravan and settled behind them.

[Exodus 33:9-10; Numbers 9:16-22; 10:11-12; Deuteronomy 31:15; 1 Corinthians 10:1]

20 Thus the cloud was between the camp of Egypt and the camp of Israel. On one side, it was a dark cloud; on the other side, it lighted up the night. Hence both groups did not 'bump' each other all night.

[Exodus 13:21-22; 40:38; Numbers 9:16; 14:14c; Deuteronomy 1:33; Nehemiah 9:12, 19; Psalms 78:14; 105:39; Isaiah 4:5]

21 Moses now held out his hand over the sea, and Jehovah pushed back the sea with a strong east wind all night, and the waters were split apart, making the seafloor a dry ground.

[Exodus 14:16; 15:8; Joshua 2:10a; Nehemiah 9:11a; Psalms 78:13; 106:9a; 136:12-13; Isaiah 51:10a; 63:12]

22 Soon the Israelites walked across the sea on dry ground, with the waters like walls on their right and on their left.

[Exodus 14:29; 15:8, 19c; Nehemiah 9:11a; Psalms 66:6b; 78:13; 106:9b; 136:14; Isaiah 11:15b; 43:16; 51:10b; 63:13; 1 Corinthians 10:1; Hebrews 11:29a]

23 But the Egyptians went in pursuit, and all of Pharaoh's war horses, chariot warriors, and army chased after them into the midst of the sea.

24 At the morning watch *(between 2 to 6 am)*, as Jehovah looked at the camp of the Egyptians from within the pillar of fire and cloud, He threw the Egyptians into panic.

25 He took the wheels off their chariots, so that they had a hard time driving them.

The Egyptians said: "Let's get away from the Israelites, Jehovah is fighting for them against us!"

[Exodus 14:14; Deuteronomy 1:30; 3:22b; 20:4; Joshua 10:14, 42; 23:10; 2 Chronicles 20:15b]

26 Finally Jehovah told Moses: "Hold out your hand over the sea, and the waters will flow back over the Egyptians, over their war horses and chariot warriors."

[Exodus 15:16; Deuteronomy 11:4]

27 At once Moses held out his hand over the sea, and the sea was back to normal at the crack of dawn. All along the Egyptians tried to escape, but Jehovah shook them off into the midst of the sea.

[Exodus 15:1, 4, 21; Psalms 136:15]

28 The waters flowed back and eventually covered the war horses, the chariot-warriors, and the army of Pharaoh who chased after them into the sea. Not one of them survived.

[Exodus 15:5a 10a; Deuteronomy 11:4; Joshua 24:7; Psalms 78:53; 106:11]

29 As for the Israelites, they walked across the sea on dry ground, with the waters like walls on their right and on their left.

[Exodus 14:22; 15:8, 19c; Nehemiah 9:11a; Psalms 66:6b; 78:13; 106:9b; 136:14; Isaiah 11:15b; 43:16; 51:10b; 63:13; 1 Corinthians 10:1; Hebrews 11:29a]

30 Thus Jehovah rescued the Israelites from the hand of the Egyptians on that day. And the Israelites saw the Egyptians lying dead on the seashore.

[Psalms 106:10]

31 After witnessing the strong hand of Jehovah in action against the Egyptians, the Israelites feared Jehovah and put faith in Him, and in Moses His servant.

[Psalms 106:12a]

CHAPTER 15

1 Then Moses and the Israelites sang this song to Jehovah, as follows:

> "I will sing to Jehovah, for He has triumphed!
> The horse and its rider He shook off into the sea!

[Exodus 14:27b; 15:4a, 21; Psalms 106:12b; 136:15]

2 Jah is my strength and my might,
> He comes to my rescue!
> He is my God, I will praise Him;
> my father's God, I will exalt Him!

[Psalms 28:7]

3 Jehovah is a warrior;

[Psalms 24:8; Isaiah 42:13; Zechariah 14:3]

> Jehovah is His name!

[Exodus 3:15b; Psalms 83:18; 102:12; 135:13; Isaiah 42:8a; Jeremiah 32:18; 33:2; Hosea 12:5; Amos 5:8, 27; 9:6]

4 He shook off Pharaoh's war chariots
> and army into the sea;
> His chariot warriors were sunk in the Red Sea.

[Exodus 14:27b; 15:1, 21; Psalms 136:15]

5 The surging waters covered them,
   down they sank to the bottom like stone.

[Exodus 14:28; 15:10; Deuteronomy 11:4; Joshua 24:7; Psalms 78:53; 106:11]

6 O Jehovah, how strong Your right hand is!
   O Jehovah, Your right hand shattered the enemy!

[Psalms 89:13; 98:1; 118:15c-16]

7 With Your matchless power,
   You can hurl down anyone
   who rises up against You.

[Isaiah 2:10]

   When You explode Your burning anger,
   it devours them like stubble.

[Isaiah 5:24; 47:14]

8 By the blast of Your breath,
   the waters were pushed back
   and stood like walls,
   the surging waters were solidified
   in the heart of the sea.

[Exodus 14:22, 29b; 2 Samuel 22:16; Psalms 18:15; 78:13b]

9 The enemy said, 'I will chase and catch up!
   I will divide the spoils and gratify myself with them!
   I will draw my sword and drive them away!'

[Exodus 14:4, 8-9, 17; Joshua 24:6]

10 But You blew with Your breath,
   and the sea covered them.
   And they sank like stone
   into the mighty waters.

[Exodus 15:5b, 16b; Nehemiah 9:11b]

11 Is there a God like You, O Jehovah,
   who is as awesomely holy as You?
   The One to be worshiped with hymns of praise,
   the One working wonders?

[Exodus 8:10c; 9:14; Deuteronomy 33:26; 1 Samuel 2:2; 2 Samuel 7:22; 1 Kings 8:23; 1 Chronicles 17:20; 2 Chronicles 6:14; Psalms 35:10; 40:5; 71:19; 86:8; 113:5; Isaiah 46:9; Jeremiah 10:6-7; Micah 7:18a]

12 You put out Your right hand,
   and the earth swallowed them.
[Hebrews 11:29b]

13 But with Your love,
   You took the people You have redeemed.
   With Your strength,
   You led them to Your holy temple.

[Exodus 15:17; 2 Samuel 7:23a; 1 Chronicles 17:21a]

14 The nations heard and they became nervous.

[Joshua 2:9-10a]

The inhabitants of Philistia were gripped with anguish.

15 The chiefs of Edom were shaken.

[Genesis 36:15; 1 Chronicles 1:51b-54]

The tyrants of Moab were paralyzed with fear.
All the residents of Canaan were demoralized.

16 Fear and scare fell on them.

[Exodus 23:27]

Because of Your mighty arm, O Jehovah,
they sank like stone,
after Your people have walked across,
after the people whom You redeemed
have walked across.

[Exodus 14:22; 15:5, 10b, 19; Nehemiah 9:11]

17 Then You will bring them
and settle them on Your legacy mountain,
a secure place You have prepared
to be Your dwelling, O Jehovah,
the temple Your very hands have built, O God!

[Exodus 15:13b; Psalms 78:54]

18 Jehovah reigns forever and ever!"

[Psalms 146:10]

19 When Pharaoh's war horses,
  with his chariot-warriors and army, went into the sea,
  Jehovah brought back the waters of the sea over them,
  after the Israelites have walked across the sea
  on dry ground."

[Exodus 14:26; 15:16; Deuteronomy 11:4]

20 Then Miriam the prophetess, Aaron's sister, took a tambourine, and all the women followed her with tambourine while dancing.

[1 Chronicles 6:3a]

21 And Miriam sang in response to the men:
  "Sing to Jehovah, for He has triumphed!
  The horse and its rider He shook off into the sea!"

[Exodus 14:27b; 15:1, 4; Psalms 136:15]

22 Not long thereafter Moses told the Israelites to leave the Red Sea, and they headed to the wilderness of Shur. They trekked through the wilderness 3 days, but they found no water.

[Numbers 33:8a; Psalms 136:16; Ezekiel 20:10]

23 Soon they reached Marah, but they could not drink its water because it was bitter. So it was named Marah *(meaning 'Bitter')*.

[Numbers 33:8b]

24 And the people complained to Moses, saying: "What are we going to drink?"

25 So he cried out to Jehovah, and Jehovah showed him a piece of wood. He threw it into the water, and the water became sweet. Then Jehovah laid rules and regulations on them to test them.

26 He said: "If you will carefully heed the voice of Jehovah your God, do what is right in His eyes, and obey His rules and keep all His regulations, I would not inflict on you any of the illnesses I had inflicted on the Egyptians. I, Jehovah, will be your Healer."

[Exodus 23:25-26; Deuteronomy 7:15; Psalms 30:2; 103:3; Hosea 11:3]

27 After that they came to Elim, where there were 12 springs of water and 70 palm trees, and they camped there by the shore.

[Numbers 33:9]

CHAPTER 16

1 Sometime later the whole Israelite community left Elim, and finally they came to the wilderness of Sin, which is between Elim and Sinai, on the 15th day of the 2nd month since their exodus from Egypt.

2 But the whole Israelite community murmured against Moses and Aaron there in the wilderness.

3 This was the litany of the Israelites to them: "Oh that we had died by Jehovah's hand in Egypt while there sitting before plates of meat and eating to our heart's content, for you've brought this whole community into this wilderness to starve to death!"

4 Jehovah then said to Moses: "I am going to rain down bread from heaven for everyone. Each one shall go out and gather only what he can consume for the day. Now let's see whether or not they will follow this instruction.

[Nehemiah 9:15a; Psalms 78:24; Matthew 6:11; John 6:31-32]

5 On the 6th day, they shall estimate how much they will take home, which should be twice as much as what they gather each day."

[Exodus 16:26, 29]

6 Hence Moses and Aaron spoke to all the Israelites: "In the evening *thank* Jehovah for taking you out of Egypt, **7** so that in the morning you will see the glory of Jehovah. For Jehovah heard your murmurings against Him. For who are we that you should murmur against?"

8 Moses went on: "Because Jehovah heard your murmurings against Him, Jehovah will give you meat in the evening and bread in the morning to your heart's content. For who are we? Your murmurings are not against us, but against Jehovah."

[Numbers 11:18; 16:11; Psalms 78:18, 29; 106:14]

9 And Moses told Aaron: "Tell the whole Israelite community to present themselves to Jehovah because He heard their murmurings.'"

10 As soon as Aaron has relayed it to the whole Israelite community, they turned towards the wilderness and they saw the glory of Jehovah in the clouds.

11 Jehovah went on to say to Moses:

12 "Because I have heard the murmurings of the Israelites, say to them, 'You will eat meat between sunset and dusk, and bread in the morning, to your heart's content, for you to know who Jehovah your God is.'"

[Exodus 3:14; 6:7b; 7:5; 9:16; 10:2; 14:4, 18; 16:12; 29:46; Nehemiah 9:10; Romans 9:17]

13 Thus quails came up and covered the camp that evening, and a layer of dew was formed around the camp in the morning.

[Numbers 11:31; Psalms 78:27-28; 105:40a]

14 When the layer of dew evaporated on the face of the earth, there were somewhat like flakes, as fine as frost, on the ground.

[Numbers 11:9; Psalms 105:40b]

15 When the Israelites saw it, not knowing what it was, they asked one another: "What is it?"

Moses answered them: "It's the bread that Jehovah has given as your food.

16 Jehovah has given this command: "Everyone is to gather according to his appetite and take home an homer for every member of his household."

17 And the Israelites did so, they went out to gather; some gathered much and some gathered little.

18 But when they measured it by the homer, he who gathered much has no excess, and he who gathered little has no lack; each one has gathered according to his appetite.

[2 Corinthians 8:15]

19 Moses told them: "Do not leave any of it till morning."

20 But they did not listen to Moses. Others left some till morning, and it bred worms and stank. Thus Moses got angry with them.

21 Every morning each one gathered only what he could consume, for it melted when the sun grew hot.

[Matthew 6:11]

22 On the 6th day, when they gathered manna twice as much, 2 homers per person, the chieftains of the community came to Moses and reported it.

23 He answered them: "That is the instruction of Jehovah, saying, 'Tomorrow observe sabbath, a holy sabbath to Jehovah. Bake what you can bake and cook what you can cook, and save what is left for the next day."

[Exodus 16:30; 31:13a, 16; 34:21b; Leviticus 19:3b, 30a; 26:2a; Deuteronomy 5:15b]

24 And when they saved for the next day, just as Moses has told, it did not smell or have maggots in it.

25 Moses said: "Eat it today because today is a sabbath to Jehovah. You will not find any of it on the ground today.

26 Six days you shall gather, but on the 7th day, which is a sabbath day, there shall be none."

[Exodus 16:5, 29]

27 However, some of the people still went out to gather on the 7th day, and therefore they found none.

28 Hence Jehovah asked Moses: "How long must the people refuse to follow my rules and regulations?

29 Come to realize that the Sabbath is Jehovah's gift to you. On the 6th day he is giving you bread good for 2 days, so that on the 7th day you can just stay home and need not leave his house."

[Exodus 16:5, 26]

30 Thus the people observed sabbath on the 7th day.

[Exodus 16:23]

31 The community of Israel called it 'Manna'. Its color was white like coriander seed, and its taste was like wafers with honey.

[Numbers 11:7]

32 Then Moses said: "Jehovah gave this command, 'Take an homer of it and keep it unto all generations, that they may see the bread I provided for you in the wilderness when I took you out of Egypt.'"

33 Hence Moses told Aaron: "Take a jar, put an homer of manna in it, and place it before Jehovah to be kept unto all generations."

[Hebrews 9:4]

34 And just as Jehovah had told through Moses, Aaron placed it before the Commandments as *a souvenir*.

35 The Israelites ate manna for 40 years until they came to a civilized land. Only manna was what ate until they came to the border of Canaan.

[Nehemiah 9:21a]

36 An homer is 1/10th of an ephah.

[Ezekiel 45:11b]

CHAPTER 17

1 At the command of Jehovah, the whole Israelite community journeyed by stages. They left the wilderness of Sin and encamped in Rephidim, but there was no water for the people to drink.

[Numbers 33:12-14a]

2 Soon the people quarreled with Moses, saying: "Give us water to drink!"

[Numbers 33:14b]

   Moses asked them: "Why do you quarrel with me? Why do you always test *(the patience of)* Jehovah?"

[Psalms 106:14; 1 Corinthians 10:9]

3 But because the people were so thirsty, they kept murmuring against Moses, saying: "Did you take us out of Egypt to make us die of thirst, we, our children, and our livestock?"

4 Finally Moses cried out to Jehovah, saying: "What am I to do with this people? A little more and they will stone me!"

[Numbers 14:10a]

5 Jehovah answered Moses: "Go to the people with some of the elders of Israel, and bring with you the rod with which you struck the Nile River. And walk with the rod in your hand.

[Numbers 20:7-8a]

6 There by the rock in Horeb I will stand in front of you. You shall strike the rock *('speak to the rock' in Numbers 20:8b)*, and water will flow from it, and the people will drink it."

[Nehemiah 9:15b; Psalms 78:15-16, 20a; 105:41; 114:8; Isaiah 48:21b; John 7:38; 1 Corinthians 10:4]

And Moses did so before the eyes of the elders of Israel.

[Numbers 20:9-11]

7 He called the place Massah *(meaning 'Test')* and Meribah *(meaning 'Quarrel')*, for there the Israelites tested *(the patience of)* Jehovah, saying, 'Is Jehovah with us or not?'

[Numbers 20:13; Deuteronomy 6:16; 9:22; 33:8b; Psalms 81:7c; 95:8; 106:32a]

8 Just then the Amalekites came and attacked the Israelites in Rephidim.

[Deuteronomy 25:17-18; 1 Samuel 15:2]

9 So Moses told Joshua: "Choose men from among us and go, fight against the Amalekites! Tomorrow I will stand on the top of the hill with the rod of God in my hand!"

[1 Samuel 15:3]

10 And just as Moses has told him, Joshua went to fight against the Amalekites, while Moses, Aaron, and Hur went to the top of the hill.

11 When Moses held up his arms, the Israelites were winning; but when he dropped his hands, the Amalekites were winning.

12 When the arms of Moses grew tired, Aaron and Hur supported his arms, one on this side and one on that side, holding his arms steady until the sun went down. More so, they brought a stone for him to sit on.

13 Thus the Amalekites were vanquished by Joshua with the edge of sword.

14 Jehovah now told Moses: "Write this in a memoir and read it to Joshua --- 'I will delete the name Amalek from under heaven."

[Numbers 24:20; Deuteronomy 25:19; 1 Chronicles 4:43]

15 And Moses made an altar and called it Jehovah-Nissi *(meaning 'Jehovah is my Banner')*,

16 saying, 'Because the Amalekites lifted a hand against the throne of Jehovah, Jah will be at war against them throughout their generations.'

CHAPTER 18

1 Now Jethro *(Reuel in Exodus 2:18 & Numbers 10:29)*, the priest of Midian and Moses' father-in-law, heard about all that God had done for Moses and for Israel His people, how Jehovah took the Israelites out of Egypt.

2 Earlier, Jethro (Moses' father-in-law) received back Zipporah (Moses' wife) after she had been sent away, **3** along with their two sons.

[Exodus 2:21; 4:25; Numbers 12:1; Acts 7:29]

The name of the one was Gershom *(meaning 'Settler')*, for he said, 'I have been a settler in a foreign land'.

[Exodus 2:22; 1 Chronicles 23:15; 26:24]

4 And the name of the other was Eliezer *(meaning 'God is my Help')*, for he said, 'The God of my father is My Deliverer, He delivered me from the sword of Pharaoh.'

[1 Chronicles 23:15]

5 So Jethro *(Reuel in Exodus 2:18 & Numbers 10:29)*, Moses' father-in-law, together with Moses' wife and sons, came to him in the wilderness where he was encamped, at the mountain of God.

6 Then he sent word to Moses: "I, Jethro, your father-in-law, is here to see you, along with your wife and your two sons."

7 At once Moses went down to meet his father-in-law. He bowed down and greeted him with a kiss. Then they asked one another how they were getting along. Afterwards they went into the tent.

8 Moses related to his father-in-law all that Jehovah had done to Pharaoh and to Egypt in behalf of Israel, and how Jehovah delivered them from all the calamities that befell them.

9 And Jethro *(Reuel in Exodus 2:18 & Numbers 10:29)* was glad to hear all the good acts that Jehovah had done for Israel, rescuing them from the hand of the Egyptians.

10 Jethro said: "Thank Jehovah for rescuing you and the people from the hand of the Egyptians and from the hand of Pharaoh.

11 Now I know that Jehovah is more powerful than all the god-kings who treated them tyrannically.

[2 Chronicles 2:5; Psalms 95:3; 97:9]

12 Then Jethro *(Reuel in Exodus 2:18 & Numbers 10:29)*, Moses' father-in-law, presented burnt offerings and animal sacrifices to God, and Aaron and all the elders of Israel came to eat with him before God.

13 The next day, as usual, Moses took his seat to serve as judge for the people, while the people were standing around him from morning till evening.

[Matthew 23:2]

14 On seeing how he was dealing with the people, Moses' father-in-law asked: "Why do you deal with the people this way? Why are you sitting alone, while all the people were standing around you from morning till evening?"

15 Moses answered his father-in-law: "The people come to me to consult God.

16 When two parties have a dispute, they come to me, and I judge between them. Then I hand down the verdict and judgment of God."

17 Moses' father-in-law said to him: "The way you're handling it is not practical.

18 You will surely wear out, both you and the people who come to you. The work is too heavy for you, you cannot do it all alone.

[Numbers 11:14; Deuteronomy 1:9, 12]

19 Now heed my advice, and God will be with you. Represent the people before God, be the one to bring their cases to Him.

20 And remind them of His rules and regulations, show them how they should walk, and what they should do.

21 Then choose from among the people qualified men --- God-fearing, trustworthy, and who hate bribe. And appoint them as chiefs of thousands, chiefs of hundreds, chiefs of fifties, and chiefs of tens.

22 They shall serve as judges for the people when the occasion arises. The difficult cases they will bring to you, but the simple cases they will decide themselves. Have them share the burden with you, and it will be lighter for you.

[Numbers 11:17]

23 If you do this, just as God tells you, you would surely last. What's more, this people can go home in peace."

24 Right away Moses heeded the voice of his father-in-law and followed his advice.

[Proverbs 12:15]

25 Moses chose qualified men from among the Israelites and appointed them as chiefs of thousands, chiefs of hundreds, chiefs of fifties, and chiefs of tens.

26 They shall serve as judges for the people when the occasion arises. The difficult cases they would bring to Moses, but the simple ones they would decide themselves.

27 After that Moses sent his father-in-law off, and he went his way back to his land.

CHAPTER 19

1 On that same day of the 3rd month since their exodus from Egypt, they arrived in the wilderness of Sinai.

2 The Israelites set out from Rephidim and encamped in the wilderness of Sinai facing the mountain *(or Mount Sinai)*.

[Numbers 33:15]

3 Moses went up to the mountain, and there Jehovah God told him: "Say this to the house of Jacob and to the Israelites, **4** 'You have seen yourselves what I did to the Egyptians so that I could carry you on eagles' wings and bring you to Me.

[Deuteronomy 1:31; 32:10-11; Isaiah 31:5a]

5 So now if you will strictly heed My voice and keep My covenant *(with you)*, you would be My legacy people, although the entire earth belongs to Me."

[Exodus 34:9; Deuteronomy 4:20; 7:6; 9:26, 29; 14:2; 26:18; 32:9; 1 Kings 8:51; Psalms 135:4; 1 Peter 2:9]

6 And you will be *kings and* priests to Me, a holy people.'

[Ezra 9:2; Isaiah 61:6a; 1 Peter 2:9a; Revelation 1:6; 5:10; 20:4b, 6]

These are the words you are to say to the Israelites."

7 Hence Moses left, called the elders of the people, and relayed to them all the words that Jehovah had told him.

8 And all the people *('elders of the people' in Verse 7)* answered unanimously: "All that Jehovah says we will do."

[Exodus 24:3, 7b]

As soon as Moses has relayed the reply of the people *('elders of the people' in Verse 7)* to Jehovah, **9** Jehovah said to Moses: "I am coming to you in a thick cloud so that the people can hear Me when I speak with you. In that way, they will also put faith in you."

10 Jehovah went on to say to Moses: "You shall go to the people and cleanse them today and tomorrow, and have them wash their clothes.

11 They must be ready by the 3rd day, because on the 3rd day I will come down on Mount Sinai before the eyes of all the people.

12 You shall set limits for the people all around *(the mountain- see Exodus 19:23)* and warn them, 'Beware, do not go up to the mountain and do not touch its base. Whoever touches the mountain shall definitely be put to death.

13 He will be stoned or shot *(with arrows)*, and no one may touch him. Whether man or beast, he shall not live. Only when the ram's horn is blown can they approach the mountain."

[Hebrews 12:20]

14 So Moses went down from the mountain, cleansed the people, and had them washed their clothes.

15 He told the people: "Prepare yourselves these 3 days. Men, do not go near a woman."

16 On the 3rd day, when the morning came, there were thunders and lightning, and a thick cloud on the mountain, and a very loud trumpet blast, making all the people in the camp trembled.

[Exodus 20:18]

17 Moses now led the people out of the camp to meet God, and they stood at the foot of the mountain.

18 When Jehovah came down in fire on Mount Sinai, the whole mountain began to shake violently and all in smoke, like smoke rising from a furnace.

[Deuteronomy 4:11; Psalms 104:32; 144:5b; Isaiah 64:3]

19 As the sound of the horn grew louder and louder, Moses spoke, and God answered him audibly.

[Deuteronomy 5:24a]

20 Jehovah came down on the top of Mount Sinai and called Moses to come over, and Moses went up.

21 But then Jehovah told Moses: "Go down, warn the people not to force their way through to Jehovah, to take a look, or many of them have to die.

[Exodus 19:24]

22 Have the priests *(elders in Verse 7)* cleanse themselves, those who regularly come near to Me, or I will break out against them."

23 Moses answered Jehovah: "The people will not come up to Mount Sinai because You have already warned us, saying, 'Set limits around the mountain and regard it as holy.'"

[Exodus 19:12a]

24 Still Jehovah told him: "You shall go down and then come up, you and Aaron. Do not let the priests *(elders in Verse 7)* and the people force their way through to come to Me, or I will break out against them."

25 Thus Moses went down to the people and warned them.

CHAPTER 20

1 Then God said the following:

2 "I, Jehovah your God, took you out of Egypt, from the land of slavery.

[Exodus 29:46; Leviticus 11:45a; 25:38a, 55; 26:45a; Numbers 15:41. 23:22; Deuteronomy 5:6; Judges 6:8; 1 Kings 8:51; 2 Kings 17:36; Psalms 81:10a; Amos 3:1]

3 Worship no any other god but Me.

[Genesis 35:2; Deuteronomy 5:7; Joshua 24:14, 23; 1 Samuel 7:3-4; 2 Kings 5:17; Daniel 3:28; Matthew 4:10; Luke 4:8]

4 Do not worship a carved image or the like of anything that is in heaven above or on the earth or in the deep below the water surface.

[Exodus 20:22-23; 32:31; 34:17; Leviticus 19:4; 26:1; Deuteronomy 4:15-19, 23; 5:8; 9:12, 16; 16:21-22; 27:15; 32:21; 1 Kings 14:9; 2 Kings 17:12; Psalms 78:58; 97:7; 106:19-20; 115:4-8; 135:15-18; Isaiah 40:19-20; 41:29; 42:8, 17; 44:9-20; 45:20; Jeremiah 2:27-28; 10:3-5, 14-15; 51:17-18; Hosea 13:2; Micah 1:7a; Nahum 1:14; Habakkuk 2:18-19; Acts 17:29-30; Revelation 9:20]

5 Do not bow down to them nor be misled to worship them, because I, Jehovah your God, demand to be worshipped alone.

[Exodus 22:20; 23:13, 24a; 32:8; 34:14; Numbers 25:11; Deuteronomy 4:24; 5:9a; 6:14-15; 11:16-17; 29:26-28; 30:17-18; 31:16-18; 32:21; Joshua 23:7; 24:19-20; 2 Kings 17:35; Psalms 81:9; Isaiah 2:8-9; 46:5-7; Jeremiah 22:8-9; 25:6; Ezekiel 5:13; 39:25; Micah 5:13; Nahum 1:2a]

I punish children for the sins of their parents up to the 3rd or 4th generation of those who hate Me; **6** but love up to the 1000th generation of those who love Me and keep My commandments.

[Exodus 34:7; Numbers 14:18; Deuteronomy 5:9b-10; 7:9-10; Jeremiah 32:18; Nahum 1:3a]

7 Do not mention 'Jehovah', the name of your God, in a bad way, for Jehovah will not leave unpunished whoever does so.
[Exodus 22:28; Leviticus 19:12; 22:32; 24:14-16; Numbers 15:30; Deuteronomy 5:11]

8 Keep the sabbath day holy.

[Exodus 16:23; 31:14a; Deuteronomy 5:12; Isaiah 56:2; 58:13; Ezekiel 44:24d]

9 Six days you may work, **10** but the 7th day is the Sabbath to Jehovah your God, on which you must not do any work, you nor your son or your daughter, nor your male slave or female slave, nor the settlers in your city or your farm animal.

[Exodus 23:12; 31:15a; 34:21a; 35:2a; Leviticus 23:3; Deuteronomy 5:13-14]

11 For after creating the heavens, the earth, the sea, and all that is in them in 6 days, Jehovah rested and was refreshed on the

7th day. That is why Jehovah blessed the sabbath day and declared it holy.

[Genesis 2:2-3; Exodus 31:17b; Hebrews 4:4]

12 Respect your father and your mother so that you may live long in the land that Jehovah your God is giving you.

[Leviticus 19:3a; Deuteronomy 5:16; 27:16; Proverbs 1:8; 4:1; 19:26; 20:20; 23:22; Matthew 15:4; 19:19a; Mark 7:10; 10:19; Luke 18:20; Ephesians 6:1-3; Colossians 3:20]

13 Do not murder.

[Deuteronomy 5:17; Matthew 5:21; 19:18; Mark 10:19; Luke 18:20; Romans 13:9; James 2:11]

14 Do not commit adultery.

[Leviticus 20:10; Deuteronomy 5:18; 22:22; Matthew 5:27; 19:18; Mark 10: 19; Luke 18:20; Romans 13:9; James 2:11]

15 Do not steal.

[Leviticus 19:11; Deuteronomy 5:19; Joshua 7:11; Matthew 19:18; Mark 10:19; Luke 18:20; Romans 2:21; 13:9a; Ephesians 4:28]

16 Do not bear false witness against your fellowman.

[Exodus 23:1-2, 7; Leviticus 19:16; Deuteronomy 5:20; Matthew 19:18; Mark 10:19; Luke 18:20]

17 Do not covet your fellowman's house or spouse, nor his male slave or female slave, nor his bull or donkey, nor anything that belongs to him."

[Deuteronomy 5:21; Mark 10:19; Romans 7:7c; 13:9]

18 Now after witnessing the roaring of thunders, the flashes of lightnings, the blasts of trumpets, and the mountain smoking, the people trembled and stood at a distance.

[Exodus 19:16]

19 And they said to Moses: "Speak with us, and we will listen, but do not have God speak with us, lest we die."

[Deuteronomy 5:27; 18:16]

20 Moses answered the people: "Do not be afraid. God has come to test you *(to stabilized your quality)* that you may ever fear Him and not sin."

[Deuteronomy 4:10]

21 And s the people stood at a distance, Moses went near the thick mass of cloud where God was.

[1 Kings 8:12; 2 Chronicles 6:1; Psalms 97:2a]

22 Jehovah went on to say to Moses: "Say this to the Israelites, 'Since you yourselves have witnessed that it was from heaven that I spoke to you, **23** you must therefore not worship gods made of gold or gods of made silver.

[Deuteronomy 4:12, 15-19; Acts 17:29-30; Revelation 9:20]

24 Make for Me an offering stand of clay on which you shall offer your flock and your herd as burnt offerings and fellowship offerings. Wherever I am given glory, I will surely go there to bless you.

25 If you make an offering stand of stone for Me, you shall not cut the stone; for when you use a tool on it, you defile it.

[Deuteronomy 27:5-6; Joshua 8:31]

26 And you shall not make an offering stand for Me with stairs, lest your private parts be exposed."

CHAPTER 21

1 And lay the following laws on them:

2 When you buy a Hebrew slave, he shall be your slave 6 years, but on the 7th year he will leave as a freeman without paying anything.

[Deuteronomy 15:12; Jeremiah 34:14a]

3 If he comes alone, he should leave alone. If he comes with a wife, he should leave with his wife.

4 If his master gives him a wife, and she bears him children, her wife and her children should belong to his master, and he shall leave alone.

5 But if the slave declares, 'I really love my master, my wife, and my children, I do not want to leave as a freeman' ---

6 then his master shall present him before God and pierce his ear with an awl to the door or to the doorpost, and he shall be his slave for life.

[Deuteronomy 15:16-17]

7 But female slaves shall not leave as male slaves do.

8 If her master is not pleased with her so that he does not designate her as a concubine, and wants to sell her, then he has no right to sell her to foreign people. Such would be tantamount to treachery.

9 In case he designates her *(as a concubine)* for his son, he shall treat her like a daughter.

10 Or in case *he marries her* and takes another wife, her food, clothing, and marital dues are not to be reduced.

11 If he will not provide her these 3 things, she should leave without paying anything.

12 Whoever kills a man is to be put to death without fail.

[Genesis 9:6; Leviticus 24:17, 21b; Numbers 35:30-31]
13 But if it is not intentional, and I let it happen in his hand, I would arrange with you a place where he can flee.

[Numbers 35:11; Deuteronomy 4:41-42; 19:3-4; Joshua 20:2-3]

14 When a man gets heated against anyone and murders him, take him, even from My altar, to die.

[1 Kings 2:29]

15 Whoever strikes his father or his mother is to be put to death without fail.

16 Whoever kidnaps a person, whether he sells him or detains him, is to be put to death without fail.

[Deuteronomy 24:7]

17 Whoever curses his father or his mother is to be put to death without fail.

[Leviticus 20:9; Proverbs 20:20; 30:17; Matthew 15:4; Mark 7:10]

18 When (2) men fight, and the one strikes the other with a stone or with his fist, but the other does not die and is confined to bed, **19** and soon gets up and walks around outside on some support, he who struck him shall go unpunished. Only he shall make compensation for the wages he lost until he fully recovers.

20 When a man strikes his slave with a rod, male or female, and he/she dies by his hand, the slave is to be avenged without fail.

21 But if the slave survives a day or two, he/she is not to be avenged because he/she is his property.

22 When (2) men fight and they hurt a pregnant woman, so that she gives birth prematurely, but without serious injury, by all means fine is to be imposed on them based on what the woman's husband stipulates on them, which they shall course through the judges.

23 But if there is serious injury, then one shall pay life for life, **24** eye for eye, tooth for tooth, hand for hand, foot for foot, **25** burn for burn, wound for wound, bruise for bruise.

[Leviticus 24:18-20; Deuteronomy 19:21; Matthew 5:38]

26 When a man hits the eye of his slave, male or female, and he damages it, he has to let him go as a freeman in compensation for his eye.

27 If it is the tooth of his slave, male or female, that he knocks out, then he has to let him go as a freeman in compensation for his tooth.

28 When a bull gores a person, male or female, and he/she dies, the bull is to be stoned to death without fail, and its meat must not to be eaten, and the bull's owner is to go unpunished.

29 But if the bull is in the habit of goring, and warning has been served to its owner, but has not kept it penned up, so that it killed a person, male or female, the bull is to be stoned to death, and its owner to be put to death.

30 If a ransom is imposed on the owner, then he shall pay whatever amount is imposed on him to redeem his life.

[Proverbs 13:8a]

31 This rule applies to owners of a bull who gored a person, male or female.

32 If the bull gored *to death* a slave, male or female, the owner shall pay 30 shekels *(or 6 pounds of silver)* to the slave's master, and the bull shall be stoned to death.

33 When a man opens or digs a pit and does not cover it, and a bull or a donkey falls into it, **34** the owner of the pit is to make compensation. He shall pay the owner its current price, and the dead animal shall be his.

35 When a bull gored another bull to death, their owners shall sell the live bull and divide the money *equally between them*, as well as the dead bull.

36 But if the bull is known to be in the habit of goring, and its owner would not keep it penned up, then he shall make compensation without fail, bull for bull, and the dead bull shall be his.

CHAPTER 22

1 When a man steals a cattle or a sheep, whether he slaughters it or sells it, he is to pay 5 cattle for 1 cattle, or 4 sheep for 1 sheep.

[2 Samuel 12:6a; Luke 19:8b]

2 If a thief was caught in the act of breaking in *(at night)* and was struck to death, there should be no bloodguilt for him.

3 But if the sun has risen on him, then there is bloodguilt for him. All the same, a thief is to make compensation by all means for the things he has stolen. If he has nothing, he should be sold.

[Matthew 18:25]

4 If what was stolen was found in his possession without a doubt, whether a cattle or a donkey or a sheep, then he shall make double compensation.

5 When a man lets his field or vineyard be grazed bare and sends his farm animals to graze in someone else's field or vineyard, he shall make compensation from the best of his own field or from the best of his vineyard.

6 When a fire breaks out and spreads to thornbushes and devours sheaves of grain or standing grain in a field, by all means the one who started the fire shall make compensation for what was burned.

7 When a man entrusts money or valuables to his friend for safekeeping, and it is stolen from his house, the thief, if caught, shall make double compensation.

8 But if the thief is not found, the keeper should be brought before God to determine whether or not he got his hands on the valuables of his friend.

9 Any case of dispute involving a cattle or a donkey or a sheep or a garment, any lost thing of which two persons claim, shall be brought before God. And the one whom God pronounces guilty shall make double compensation to the owner.

10 When a man entrusts a donkey or a cattle or a sheep or any domestic animal to someone for safekeeping, and it dies or gets crippled or strayed away while no one is looking, **11** the keeper shall take an oath by Jehovah that he did not get his hands on his friend's property, and therefore need not make compensation, and the owner must believe it.

12 If it was found out that he has stolen it, then he shall make compensation to the owner.

13 But if it was mangled by a wild beast, the keeper should bring the carcass as evidence; for he is not to make compensation for what was mangled by a wild beast.

14 When someone borrows an animal from his neighbor, and it gets crippled or dies while away from its owner, by all means the borrower shall make compensation.

15 If the owner is with it, he should not make compensation. If it is rented, the loss is covered by the rental fee.

16 When a man seduces and sleeps with a virgin who is single, he shall marry her without fail and pay the bride-price.

[Genesis 34:12a; Deuteronomy 22:28-29]

17 If her father refuses outright to marry her off to him, then he shall pay an amount equivalent to the bride-price for virgins.

[Deuteronomy 22:29a]

18 You shall not spare the life of a witch.

[Leviticus 20:27]

19 Whoever mates with an animal shall definitely be put to death.

[Leviticus 20:15-16]

20 Whoever offers a sacrifice to any god other than Jehovah is to be doomed to destruction.

[Deuteronomy 13:12-15]

21 Do not mistreat nor oppress a settler, for you were once settlers in Egypt.

[Exodus 23:9; Leviticus 19:33]

22 Do not oppress widows and orphans.

23 If ever you oppress anyone of them, and he/she cries out to me, by all means I would hear his outcry.

24 I will explode in anger and kill you with sword. And your wife will become widow and your children orphans.

[Psalms 109:9]

25 When you lend money to My people, to the needy among you, do not be like a loan shark to them; do not charge interest on them.

[Leviticus 25:36-37; Deuteronomy 23:19-20]

26 If you take the garment of someone as collateral, then return it to him when the sun goes down.

[Deuteronomy 24:13, 17b]

27 That is his only covering, with what will he sleep in? In case he cries out to me, I would hear because I am compassionate.

28 Do not curse God or anyone in authority among your people.

[Leviticus 24:15; Ecclesiastes 10:20; Acts 23:5b]

29 Do not hesitate to offer the produce of your overflowing presses.

[Deuteronomy 18:4; 2 Chronicles 31:5; Proverbs 3:9-10]

Give to Me your firstborn son.

[Exodus 13:2, 12a; 22:29b; 34:19a; Numbers 18:15a]

30 Do the same with your calf and lamb. They will stay with their mother 7 days, but on the 8th day give them to Me.

[Leviticus 22:27]

31 Keep yourselves clean in My eyes.

[Leviticus 11:44b-45; 19:2; 20:7, 26; Numbers 15:40; 1 Peter 1:15-16]

And you must not eat the meat of any animal that has been mangled by a wild beast, throw it to dogs.

[Leviticus 22:8; Deuteronomy 14:21a]

CHAPTER 23

1 Do not give untrue testimony. Do not conspire with someone wicked to be a witness to a fabricated violence.

[Leviticus 19:16; Psalms 15:1-3; Proverbs 6:16-19]

2 Do not follow the majority for evil ends. Do not testify in a trial so as to conspire with the majority in perverting justice.

[Deuteronomy 16:19a]

3 Do not show bias towards a lowly person's lawsuit.

[Leviticus 19:15; Deuteronomy 1:17a; Job 32:21a; Proverbs 18:5; 24:23; 28:21a]

4 If by chance you find your enemy's cattle or donkey straying away, bring it back to him without fail.

[Deuteronomy 22:1]

5 When you see the donkey of someone who hates you collapsing under heavy load, do not just walk by, get it loose without fail.

[Deuteronomy 22:4]

6 Do not deprive justice to a poor person in his lawsuit.

7 Keep far from an untrue testimony. Do not put the innocent and the righteous to death, for never will I pronounce the wicked righteous.

[Deuteronomy 25:1; 1 Kings 8:32; Proverbs 17:15]

8 Do not accept bribe, for bribe blinds the clearsighted and makes the righteous twist their words.

[Deuteronomy 16:19b; Proverbs 15:27; 17:23; Ecclesiastes 7:7b]

9 Do not oppress settlers. You yourselves know how it is to be a settler, for you were once settlers in Egypt.

[Exodus 22:21; Leviticus 19:33]

10 For 6 years sow your field with seed and reap its harvest.

[Leviticus 25:3]

11 But in the 7th year leave it uncultivated and let it lie fallow. Let the poor of your people eat of it, and let the wild beasts eat what is left of them. Do the same with your vineyard and with your olive grove.

[Leviticus 25:4]

12 Six days you may work, but rest on the 7th day, so that your slaves and the settlers may refresh themselves, as well as your cattle and donkey.

[Exodus 20:9-10; 31:15a; 34:21a; 35:2a; Leviticus 23:3; Deuteronomy 5:13-14]

13 Do not mention the name of other gods; it should not be heard from you.

[Joshua 23:7b]

Bear in mind all that I have told you.

14 Celebrate 3 annual feasts to Me.

[Exodus 23:17; 34:23; Deuteronomy 16:16; 2 Chronicles 8:13]

15 *First,* commemorate the Feast of Unleavened Bread.

[Exodus 12:17; 34:18; Leviticus 23:6a; Deuteronomy 16:16; 2 Chronicles 8:13; 30:21; 35:17; Ezra 6:22a; Ezekiel 45:21b; Luke 22:1; Acts 12:3b; 1 Corinthians 5:8]

Just as I have told you, eat unleavened bread 7 days at the scheduled time and date in the month of Abib, on which you came out of Egypt. And do not appear before Me empty-handed.

[Exodus 12:18; 34:18b, 20d; Leviticus 23:6; Numbers 28:17]

16 *Second,* the Feast of Harvest *('Festival of Weeks' in Exodus 34:22a, while 'Festival of Pentecost' in Acts 2:1),* when you reap the firstfruits of your labor from what you have planted in the field.

[Numbers 28:26; Deuteronomy 16:10; 2 Chronicles 8:13]

And *third,* the Feast of Ingathering *(Festival of Booths in Exodus 34:22b, Leviticus 23:34, Deuteronomy 16:13, Ezra 3:4, Nehemiah 8:14 & Zechariah 14:16, and Festival of Tabernacles in*

John 7:2) at the end of the year, when you gather in *the fruit of* your labor from the field.

[2 Chronicles 8:13]

17 On these 3 annual occasions every male of yours shall appear before God.

[Exodus 23:14; 34:23; Deuteronomy 16:16; 2 Chronicles 8:13b]

18 Do not serve the meat of My Passover sacrifice along with anything made with yeast. And do not leave any of it till morning.

[Exodus 12:8, 10a; 34:25; Leviticus 7:15; 22:30b; Numbers 9:11b-12a; Deuteronomy 16:3a]

19 Bring the best of the firstfruits of your soil to the temple of Jehovah your God.

[Exodus 34:26a; Leviticus 2:12; 23:10; Deuteronomy 26:2; Nehemiah 10:35; Proverbs 3:9; Ezekiel 44:30]

Do not boil a baby goat in the milk of its mother.

[Exodus 34:26b; Deuteronomy 14:21d]

20 I will send *My* angel ahead of you to protect you along the way and to bring you into the place I have prepared.

[Genesis 48:16a; Exodus 3:2; 14:19a; 32:34b; Isaiah 63:9b; Acts 7:30, 35b]

21 Be careful to heed his voice. Do not be unruly, for he will not condone your rebellious behavior. He acts in My name.

22 If you carefully heed his voice and do all that I say, I would be hostile to your enemies and would harass those who harass you.

23 My angel will go ahead of you and bring you to the *territory of the* Amorites, Hittites, Perizzites, Canaanites, Hivites, and Jebusites, whom I will wipe off the face of the earth.

[Exodus 33:2]

24 Do not bow down to their gods nor be misled to worship them. Do not imitate what they do. Instead, pull down *their offering stands (see Exodus 34:13)* and break their idolatrous posts into pieces.

[Exodus 34:13; Leviticus 18:3; Deuteronomy 7:5; 12:3; Judges 2:2b; 2 Kings 10:27; 11:18a; 23:14-15; 2 Chronicles 14:3; 31:1a; 34:4a, 7a]

25 Worship Jehovah your God, and He would purify your food and water, and remove sickness from your midst.

[Deuteronomy 7:15; Psalms 103:3]

26 No woman will miscarry nor there will be a barren woman in your land. I will make you live your life to the full.

[Deuteronomy 7:14b]

27 I will send scare of Me ahead of you, I will throw into panic all the people you encounter, and I will give you the nape of the necks of all your enemies.

[Genesis 49:8b; Deuteronomy 2:25; 7:20; 11:25; Joshua 2:9, 24b; 10:24b; 2 Samuel 22:41; 2 Chronicles 20:29; Psalms 18:40]

28 I will send terror ahead of you, and it will drive out the Hivites, the Canaanites, and the Hittites from before you.

[Exodus 34:11b; Psalms 80:8b]

29 But I will not drive them out from before you in a year's time, lest the land become desolate and the wild beasts become too many for you.

30 I will drive them out from before you gradually, until you become many enough to occupy the land.

[Deuteronomy 7:22; Joshua 23:13; Judges 2:3a, 23; Psalms 105:44]

31 I will define your borders, from the Red Sea to the Philistine Sea, and from the wilderness to the River *(Yarkon)*. I will give the inhabitants of the land into your hand so that you can drive them out from before you.

32 Do not make a treaty with them or with their god-*kings*.

[Exodus 34:12a; Deuteronomy 7:2c; Judges 2:2a; Psalms 106:35]

33 For if they dwell in your land, they would make you sin against Me. And once you worship their gods, you are hooked."

[Deuteronomy 7:16b, 25; Judges 2:3b; Psalms 106:36]

CHAPTER 24

1 Then Jehovah said to Moses: "Come up, you, Aaron, Nadab, Abihu, and 70 of the elders of Israel, and worship Me at a distance.

[Numbers 11:16; Ezekiel 8:11a; Luke 10:1]

2 You alone may approach Me, but they may not. And the people may not come up with you."

3 So Moses left and relayed all the words of Jehovah and all His laws to the people, and all of them answered unanimously: "All that Jehovah says we will do."

[Exodus 19:8a; 24:7b]

4 Hence Moses wrote down all the words of Jehovah (*'the Commandments' in Exodus 34:28*).

[Exodus 34:27; Deuteronomy 27:8]

Then early in the morning he made an offering stand at the foot of the mountain and set up 12 pillars representing the 12 tribes of Israel.

[1 Kings 18:31; Revelation 21:12]

5 After that he sent Israelite attendants to present bull calves as burnt offerings and fellowship sacrifices to Jehovah.

6 Then Moses poured half of the blood in a basin and spattered the other half all over the offering stand.

7 Finally he took the scroll of the Commandments and read it aloud *to* the people.

[2 Kings 23:2b]

   And they answered: "All that Jehovah says we will do and obey."

[Exodus 19:8a; 24:3]

8 Then Moses took the blood, spattered it on the people, and said: "This is the blood of the covenant that Jehovah has made with you based on these words.

[Matthew 26:28; Hebrews 9:15-22]

9 Afterwards Moses, Aaron, Nadab, Abihu, and 70 of the elders of Israel came up, **10** and they saw the God of Israel, under whose feet was somewhat like a pavement of sapphire as clear as the sky.

11 Although the distinguished men of Israel saw God, He did not put out His hand against them. Hence they ate and drank.

12 Jehovah now told Moses: "Come up to Me in the mountain and wait there, for I am going to give you the stone tablets on which I wrote the Commandments and the Laws you are to teach them."

[Exodus 31:18; 32:16; 34:1; Deuteronomy 4:13-14; 5:22; 9:10; 10:1-4]

13 Before Moses and Joshua his assistant went up to the mountain of God,

14 *Moses* told the elders: "Wait for us here until we return to you. Aaron and Hur are here with you; whoever has a dispute may go to them."

15 Then Moses went up to the cloud-covered mountain.

16 The glory of Jehovah settled on the cloud-covered Mount Sinai 6 days, and finally on the 7th day He called Moses from the midst of the cloud.

[1 Kings 8:12; 2 Chronicles 6:1]

17 (To the Israelites, the glory of Jehovah on the mountaintop looked like a raging fire.)

[Deuteronomy 4:24a; Hebrews 12:29]

18 Then Moses entered the cloud-covered mountain and stayed there 40 days and 40 nights.

[Exodus 20:21; Deuteronomy 9:9b; 10:10a]

CHAPTER 25

1 Then Jehovah said to Moses:

2 "Tell the Israelites to accept for Me what anyone is willing to give.

3 You may receive from them the following:

   gold, silver, and bronze **[Exodus 35:5]**

4 blue, purple, and red yarns, fine linen, and goat hair **[Exodus 35:6]**

5 tanned sheepskins, seal fur, and acacia wood **[Exodus 35:7]**

6 oil for light, and spice extracts for the anointing oil and for the scented incense **[Exodus 35:8]**

7 onyx stones and gemstones to be set on the ephod and on the breastplate **[Exodus 35:9]**

8 And they shall build a tabernacle for Me, where I will dwell among them.

[1 Corinthians 3:16]

9 Make the tabernacle and all its furnishings in accordance with the pattern I will show you.

[Exodus 25:40; 26:30; Acts 7:44; Hebrews 8:5b]

10 Make a Box of acacia wood, 3.75 feet long, 2.25 feet wide, and 2.25 feet high.

[Exodus 37:1]

11 Coat it with pure gold, inside out, and make a gold molding around it.

[Exodus 37:2]

12 Cast 4 rings of gold and attach them above its 4 feet, with 2 rings on either side.

[Exodus 37:3]

13 Make *(2)* poles of acacia wood and coat them with gold.

[Exodus 37:4]

14 Insert the poles into the rings on either side of the Box with which to carry it.

[Exodus 37:5]

15 The poles are to remain inserted into the rings of the Box; they are not to be removed from them.

16 Put the Commandments, which I will give you, in the Box.

[Exodus 40:20a]

17 Make a cover of pure gold, 3.75 feet long and 2.25 feet wide.

[Exodus 37:6]

18 Make 2 cherubs of hammered gold and place them on the 2 ends of the cover.

[Exodus 37:7]

19 Put the one cherub on one end and the other cherub on the other end.

[Exodus 37:8]

20 The two wings of each cherub are to spread forward to screen off the cover, with the cherubs facing each other and their eyes toward the cover.

[Exodus 37:9]

21 After you have put the Commandments in the Box, which I will give you, put its cover.

[Exodus 40:20]

22 For from above the cover, between the 2 cherubs on the Box of the Commandments, I will meet with you and speak with you in behalf of the Israelites.

[Exodus 30:6; Leviticus 16:2b; Numbers 7:89; 17:4; Judges 20:27; 2 Samuel 6:2; 2 Kings 19:15; 1 Chronicles 13:6; Psalms 80:1b; 99:1b]

23 Make a table of acacia wood, 3 feet long, 1.5 feet wide, and 2.5 feet high.

[Exodus 37:10]

24 Coat it with pure gold and make a gold molding around it.

[Exodus 37:11]

25 Make a rim around it, the span of a hand, and make a gold molding around the rim.

[Exodus 37:12]

26 Cast 4 rings of gold and attach them to the 4 corners above its 4 feet.

[Exodus 37:13]

27 The rings are to be close to the rim to hold the carrying poles.

[Exodus 37:14]

28 Make poles of acacia wood, with which to carry the table, and coat them with gold.

[Exodus 37:15]

29 Make plates, cups, pitchers, and bowls of pure gold.

[Exodus 37:16]

30 And set showbread on the table before Me at all times.

[Exodus 40:4, 23]

31 Make a lampstand of pure hammered gold, to be of one piece with its base and *decorative* branches, calyxes, and flower knobs.

[Exodus 37:17]

32 Six branches are to extend from the sides of the lampstand; 3 branches on one side and 3 branches on the other side.

[Exodus 37:18]

33 Three cups shaped like almond flowers are to be on every branch on the one side, and under every cup their flower knobs. Likewise, 3 cups shaped like almond flowers on every branch on the other side, and under every cup their flower knobs. That is how it is for the 6 branches extending from the lampstand.

[Exodus 37:19]

34 But on the lampstand shaft 4 cups shaped like almond flowers on every branch, and under every cup their flower knobs.

[Exodus 37:20]

35 Two flower knobs under every cup on the one side, and 2 flower knobs under every cup on the other side. That is how it is for the 6 branches extending from the lampstand.

[Exodus 37:21]

36 All the flower knobs and the branches extending from the lampstand are to be of one piece with it, all of hammered pure gold.

[Exodus 37:22]

37 Make 7 lamps for it, and direct their light towards the front area.

[Exodus 37:23a]

38 And their wick trimmers and fire holders are to be of pure gold.

[Exodus 37:23b]

39 Use one talent *(or 75 pounds)* of pure gold in making it and all its accessories.

40 See to it that you make them in accordance with their pattern that was shown to you on the mountain."

[Exodus 25:9; 26:30; Acts 7:44; Hebrews 8:5b]

CHAPTER 26

1 "Make a tabernacle of 10 wall tents using blue, purple and red fine twisted linen, and embroider cherubs on them.

[Exodus 36:8]

2 All the wall tents have the same measure --- 42 feet long by 6 feet wide.

[Exodus 36:9]

3 Join the 5 wall tents into one set, and the other 5 into another set.

[Exodus 36:10]

4 Make loops of blue yarn along the edge of the end wall tent in the one set, and do the same in the other set.

[Exodus 36:11]

5 Make 50 loops on the end wall tent in the one set, and another 50 loops in the other set, with the loops aligned to one another.

[Exodus 36:12]

6 Cast 50 hooks of gold with which to couple the *(2 sets of)* wall tents into one tabernacle.

[Exodus 36:13]

7 And make 11 roof tents of goat hair for the tabernacle.

[Exodus 36:14]

8 All the 11 roof tents have the same measure --- 45 feet long by 6 feet wide.

[Exodus 36:15]

9 Join the 5 roof tents into one set and the 6 roof tents into another set, and leave the half of the 6th roof tent hanging over the front of the tabernacle.

[Exodus 36:16]

10 Make 50 loops along the edge of the end roof tent in the one set, and another 50 loops in the other set.

[Exodus 36:17]

11 Cast 50 hooks of bronze and put the hooks in the loops to couple the *(2 sets of)* roof tents into one roof.

[Exodus 36:18]

12 Leave the other half of the 6th roof tent hanging over the back of the tabernacle.

[Exodus 26:9]

13 The roof tents left hanging over the 2 sides of the tabernacle are to be 1.5 feet wider.

14 Make an inner roof top tent of tanned sheepskins and an outer roof top tent of seal fur for the tabernacle.

[Exodus 36:19]

15 Make upright panel frames of acacia wood for the tabernacle.

[Exodus 36:20]

16 Each panel frame is 15 feet long and 2.25 feet wide.

[Exodus 36:21]

17 Each panel frame has 2 fitting tenons. That is how you shall make all the panel frames for the tabernacle.

[Exodus 36:22]

18 Make 20 panel frames for the south side of the tabernacle.

[Exodus 36:23]

19 Make 40 baseplates of silver to go under the 20 panel frames --- 2 baseplates under every panel frame that has 2 fitting tenons.

[Exodus 36:24]

20 For the north side of the tabernacle, twenty panel frames, **21** and forty baseplates of silver --- two baseplates under every panel frame.

[Exodus 36:25-26]

22 For the west side of the tabernacle, at the back, make 6 panel frames.

[Exodus 36:27]

23 And make 2 panel frames as corner connectors for the 2 corners at the back of the tabernacle.

[Exodus 36:28]

24 The corner connectors are coupled at the top and at the bottom with a single ring each.

[Exodus 36:29]

25 In all, 8 panel frames and 16 baseplates of silver *(for the west side)* --- 2 baseplates under each panel frame.

[Exodus 36:30]

26 And make 5 crossbars of acacia wood for the panel frames on the one *(south)* side of the tabernacle; **27** another 5 crossbars for the panel frames on the other *(north)* side, and another 5 crossbars for the panel frames on the west side, and for the 2 corner connectors at the back of the tabernacle.

[Exodus 36:31-32]

28 The middle crossbar is to run from end to end at the center of the panel frames.

[Exodus 36:33]

29 Coat the panel frames and the crossbars with gold, and cast rings of gold to hold the crossbars.

[Exodus 36:34]

30 Set up the tabernacle in accordance with the pattern shown to you in the mountain.

[Exodus 25:9, 40; Acts 7:44; Hebrews 8:5b]

31 Make a curtain of blue, purple, and red fine twisted linen, and embroider cherubs on it.

[Exodus 36:35]

32 Hang it on the 4 posts of gold-coated acacia that are on 4 baseplates of silver; their hooks are of gold.

[Exodus 36:36]

33 Hang the curtain with the hooks and bring the Box of the Commandments beyond the curtain that separates the Holy Place from the Most Holy Place *(otherwise known as Holy of Holies)*.

[Exodus 30:6a; 40:3, 21; 1 Kings 6:19; 8:6; Hebrews 9:3-4]

34 But before you bring the Box of the Commandments into the Most Holy Place, put its cover first.

[Exodus 25:21]

35 Outside the curtain *(or in the Holy Place)*, place the table on the north side, and the lampstand opposite it, on the south side.

[Exodus 40:22, 24; Hebrews 9:2]

36 For the entrance of the tabernacle, make a curtain of blue, purple, and red fine twisted linen.

[Exodus 36:37]

37 For this curtain, make 5 posts of acacia, coat them with gold, and cast 5 baseplates of bronze for them; their hooks are gold."

[Exodus 36:38]

CHAPTER 27

1 "Make an offering stand *(for burnt offerings)* of acacia wood. The offering stand should be square, 7.5 feet long, 7.5 feet wide, and 4.5 feet high.

[Exodus 38:1]

2 Make horns *(or projections)* on its 4 corners, to be of one piece with it, and coat it with bronze.

[Exodus 38:2]

3 Make ash buckets, shovels, basins, forks, and fire holders. Make all these utensils of bronze.

[Exodus 38:3]

4 For it, make a grill of bronze, net design pattern, and cast 4 rings of bronze to be attached to its 4 corners.

[Exodus 38:4a, 5]

5 Install the grill at the center of the offering stand, under the ledge.

[Exodus 38:4b]

6 For this offering stand, make poles of acacia wood and coat them with bronze.

[Exodus 38:6]

7 Insert these poles into the rings on either side of the offering stand with which to carry it.

[Exodus 38:7a]

8 Make them of hollow planks, just as He had shown to you in the mountain.

[Exodus 38:7b]

9 Then make *wall tents for* the courtyard of the tabernacle.
   For the south side, the courtyard wall tents are of fine twisted linen, 150 feet long.

[Exodus 38:9, 16]

10 Their 20 posts and 20 baseplates are of bronze; the posts' hooks and fasteners are of silver.

[Exodus 38:10]

11 The same for the north side, the wall tents are 150 feet long. Their 20 posts and 20 baseplates are of bronze; the posts' hooks and fasteners are of silver.

[Exodus 38:11]

12 For the west side of the courtyard, the wall tents are 75 feet long; their posts 10 and their baseplates 10.

[Exodus 38:12]

13 For the east side of the courtyard, the wall tents are 75 feet long.

[Exodus 38:13]

14 For the one side of the entrance, the wall tents are 22.5 feet long; their posts 3 and their baseplates 3.

[Exodus 38:14]

15 And so for the other side of the entrance, the wall tents are 22.5 feet long; their posts 3 and their baseplates 3.

[Exodus 38:15]

16 For the entrance of the courtyard, weave a curtain, 30 feet long, of blue, purple, and red linen twisted yarns; their posts 4 and their baseplates 4.

[Exodus 38:18-19a]

17 All the fasteners and hooks of the posts all around the courtyard are of silver, but their baseplates are of bronze.

[Exodus 38:19b]

18 The measurement of the courtyard wall tents are 150 feet long and 7.5 feet high, of fine twisted linen, and their baseplates of bronze.

[Exodus 27:9b, 11a]

19 All the accessories of the tabernacle, whatever they maybe, and all the tent pins of the tabernacle and of the courtyard are of bronze.

[Exodus 38:20]

20 Now tell the Israelites to bring you pure virgin olive oil for light, to keep the lamps burning.

[Leviticus 24:2]

21 In the Holy Place, outside the curtain that screens off the Commandments, Aaron and his sons shall keep them lit before Jehovah from evening till morning. This is a lasting ordinance to be carried out by the Israelites throughout their generations."

[Leviticus 24:3]

CHAPTER 28

1 "As for you, take with you Aaron your brother from among the Israelites so he can serve as priest to Me, together with his sons Nadab, Abihu, Eleazar, and Ithamar.

[Exodus 6:23b; 28:1; Numbers 3:2-3; 26:60; 1 Chronicles 6:3b; 24:1]

2 For glory and beauty, make sacred garments for Aaron your brother.

3 Tell all the skilled ones, whom I have given wisdom, to make garments for Aaron with which to sanctify him so he can serve as priest to Me.

[Exodus 31:10; 35:19; 39:41]

4 They shall make the following garments: breastplate, ephod *(like an apron)*, sleeveless robe, checkered coat, turban, and sash. They shall make these sacred garments for Aaron your brother and for his sons so they can serve as priests to Me.

[Exodus 28:41; 31:10; 35:19; 39:41; 40:13-15]

5 They shall use gold, blue, purple, and red fine linen yarns.

[Exodus 39:1a]

6 They shall weave the ephod in gold, blue, purple, and red fine twisted linen.

[Exodus 39:2]

7 It shall have (2) shoulder straps that can be tied-up.

[Exodus 39:4]

8 The sash, for holding up, are of the same materials, of gold, blue, purple, and red fine twisted linen.

[Exodus 39:5]

9 Engrave on the 2 onyx stones the names of Israel's sons; **10** six names on the one stone, and the other 6 names on the other stone, in the order of their birth.

[Exodus 39:6b]

11 As a gem cutter engraves a seal, so engrave the names of Israel's sons on the 2 stones which are to be mounted in gold filigree settings.

[Exodus 39:6a]

12 Fasten the 2 onyx stones on the shoulder straps of the ephod as reminder stones. Thus Aaron shall ever bear their names on his 2 shoulder straps with which to remind Jehovah of Israel's sons.

[Exodus 39:7]

13 Make gold filigree settings, **14** and 2 ropelike chains of pure gold to hold the settings.

[Exodus 28:22]

15 Like the ephod, weave the breastplate of judgment in gold, blue, purple, and red linen twisted yarns.

[Exodus 39:8]

16 It should be square when folded, which length and width like the span of a hand.

[Exodus 39:9]

17 Then mount on it 4 rows of gemstones, as follows:

The 1st row is of ruby, topaz, and emerald.

[Exodus 39:10]

18 The 2nd row is of turquoise, sapphire, and jasper.

[Exodus 39:11]

19 The 3rd row is of leshem, agate, and amethyst.

[Exodus 39:12]

20 And the 4th row is of chrysolite, onyx, and jade.

Mount them in gold filigree settings.

[Exodus 39:13]

21 The names of Israel's 12 sons should be engraved on the onyx stones like a seal *representing* the 12 tribes of Israel.

[Exodus 39:14]

22 Encircle the breastplate with the *(2)* ropelike chains of pure gold.

[Exodus 39:15]

23 Cast 2 rings of gold to be attached to the 2 *upper* ends of the breastplate.

[Exodus 39:16]

24 Insert in layer the 2 ropelike chains of gold into the 2 rings on the *upper* ends of the breastplate.

[Exodus 39:17]

25 Then tie the ends of the 2 ropelike chains to the 2 filigree settings that are attached to the ephod's 2 shoulder straps at the front.

[Exodus 39:18]

26 Make 2 rings of gold and attach them to the 2 *lower* ends of the breastplate, to be tucked in beneath the ephod.

[Exodus 39:19]

27 Make another 2 rings of gold and attach them to the ephod's 2 shoulder straps from below, at the front near the seam, above the sash of the ephod.

[Exodus 39:20]

28 To hold up the breastplate above the sash of the ephod and not come loose atop the ephod, tie the breastplate to the ephod by their rings with a blue ribbon.

[Exodus 39:21]

29 Thus Aaron shall ever bear the names of Israel's sons on the breastplate of judgment over his heart whenever he enters the Most Holy Place as a constant reminder before Jehovah.

[Exodus 28:12]

30 Put the Urim *(indicating 'Guilty')* and the Thummim *(indicating 'Innocent')* on the breastplate of judgment, which shall ever be over Aaron's heart when he comes in before Jehovah. At the same time, Aaron shall ever bear the judgments for the Israelites over his heart before Jehovah.

[Leviticus 8:8; Deuteronomy 33:8a; Ezra 2:63]

31 Make the sleeveless robe of the ephod all in blue yarn.

[Exodus 39:22]

32 To keep its neck hole from tearing, put a woven collar around it, like the collar of a scale armor.

[Exodus 39:23]

33 Sew pomegranates of blue, purple, and red yarns around the lower hem of the sleeveless robe, with bells of gold in between them, 34 that is, a golden bell and a pomegranate alternating around its lower hem.

[Exodus 39:24-26]

35 Aaron shall wear it whenever he *burns incense* before Jehovah, so that its tinkling could be heard every time he enters and leaves the Most Holy Place, that he may not die.

[Exodus 28:43]

36 Make a shiny plate of pure gold like a seal, and engrave on it 'JEHOVAH IS HOLY'.

[Exodus 39:30]

37 Tie it to the front of the turban with a blue ribbon.

[Exodus 39:31]

38 It shall always be on the forehead of Aaron, who shall be held liable for any fault committed against the things dedicated by the Israelites. It shall ever be on his forehead so that Jehovah will accept their holy offerings.

39 Weave a checkered coat of fine linen, a turban of fine linen, and a sash.

[Exodus 39:27-28a, 29]

40 For glory and beauty, make *sleeveless* robes, sashes, and turbans for the sons of Aaron.

41 Put them on Aaron your brother and on his sons, and anoint them, ordain them, and sanctify them so they can serve as priests to Me.

[Exodus 28:4; 40:13-15; Leviticus 8:30]

42 Make linen shorts for them, from waist to thigh, with which to cover their private parts.

[Exodus 39:28b; Leviticus 6:10a; 16:4; Ezekiel 44:17-18]

43 Aaron and his sons shall wear them whenever they enter the tabernacle or whenever they burn incense in the Most Holy Place, lest they incur sin and die. That is a lasting ordinance for him and his descendants."

CHAPTER 29

1 This is how to sanctify them so they can serve as priests to Me: Take one bull calf and two male sheep, all without defect, **2** along with loaves of unleavened bread, unleavened round cakes smeared with oil, and unleavened wafers brushed with oil. Make them of fine wheat flour.

3 Present them in a basket, along with the bull calf and the two male sheep.

4 Then you shall present Aaron and his sons at the entrance of the Most Holy Place and there wash them with water.

[Leviticus 8:6]

5 You shall put on Aaron the sleeveless robe, the *checkered* coat, the ephod, the breastplate, which is to be tied tightly to him with the sash of the ephod.

[Leviticus 8:7]

6 Set the turban on his head and fasten the label of holiness on the turban.

[Leviticus 8:9]

7 Then you shall anoint him by pouring the anointing oil on his head.

[Leviticus 8:12]

8 Next you shall present his sons and put the robes on them.

[Leviticus 8:13a]

9 Afterwards you shall tie the sashes to Aaron and his sons and set the turbans on their heads. Thus you ordain Aaron and his sons, qualifying them to serve as priests *as long as they live.*

[Exodus 30:30; 40:15; Leviticus 8:13b]

10 Now present the bull calf at the entrance of the tabernacle, and Aaron and his sons shall lay their hands on its head.

[Leviticus 8:14]

11 There at the entrance of the tabernacle you shall slaughter the bull calf before Jehovah.

[Leviticus 8:15a]

12 You shall rub with your fingers some of the calf's blood on all the horns of the offering stand, and pour the remaining blood on its base.

[Leviticus 8:15b]

13 Then you shall remove all the fat blanketing the intestines and the fat on the lobes of the liver and on the 2 kidneys, and roast them on the offering stand.

[Leviticus 8:16]

14 But burn the calf's flesh, its skin, and its intestines outside the camp as a sin offering.

[Leviticus 8:17]

15 Then take one of the male sheep, and Aaron and his sons shall lay their hands on its head.

[Leviticus 8:18]

16 You shall slaughter the sheep and spatter its blood all over the offering stand.

[Leviticus 8:19]

17 You shall cut the sheep into parts, match the parts to one another up to its head, and wash its entrail and legs.

[Leviticus 8:20a]

18 Then you shall roast the sheep as whole on the offering stand for burnt offerings as a sweet-savory roasted offering to Jehovah.

[Leviticus 8:20b-21]

19 Next you shall take the other male sheep, and Aaron and his sons shall lay their hands on its head.

[Leviticus 8:22]

20 Slaughter the sheep and rub some of its blood on the lobes of the right ears of Aaron and his sons, on the thumbs of their right hands, and on the big toes of their right feet, and spatter *(some of)* the blood all over the offering stand.

[Leviticus 8:23-24]

21 Then you shall take the remaining blood from the offering stand, and some of the anointing oil, and spatter these on Aaron and his garments, and on his sons and their garments, thus making him and his garments, and his sons and their garments holy.

[Leviticus 8:30]

22 Then you shall take all the fat of the male sheep --- the fat tail, the fat blanketing the intestines, the fat on the lobes of liver and on the 2 kidneys, and the right leg, for it is a sheep for ordination; **23** as well as the loaf of unleavened bread, the round cake smeared with oil, and the wafer from the basket that is before Jehovah.

[Leviticus 8:25-26a]

24 You shall hand all of these to Aaron and his sons, and then you wave them as a wave offering before Jehovah.

[Leviticus 8:27]

25 Afterwards you shall take all of those from their hands and roast them on the offering stand for burnt offerings as a sweet-savory roasted offering to Jehovah.

[Leviticus 8:28]

26 Then you shall take the breast of the sheep of ordination, which is for Aaron, and wave it as a wave offering before Jehovah, and it shall be your share.

[Leviticus 8:29]

27 You shall sanctify the holy parts, the breast *that was waved* and the leg *that was pulled out,* those which were taken from the sheep of ordination for Aaron and for his sons.

[Leviticus 7:34; 9:21; 10:14-15]

28 These holy parts shall be the share of Aaron and his sons by a lasting ordinance to be complied by the Israelites. The Israelites shall pull out these holy parts from their fellowship sacrifices to Jehovah.

29 Hand down the sacred garments of Aaron to his son who will succeed him; anoint him and ordain him while wearing them.

[Numbers 20:26a]

30 His son who succeeds him as *high* priest and who enters the Most Holy Place to burn incense shall wear them 7 days.

[Exodus 29:35]

31 Then you shall roast the meat of the sheep of ordination in a holy place.

[Leviticus 8:31a]

32 And Aaron and his sons shall eat the meat of the sheep and the bread from the basket at the courtyard of the tabernacle.

[Leviticus 8:31b]

33 To ordain and sanctify them, they shall eat of the sacrifices by which to take away sins. But no *non-Aaronite* may eat of them because they are holy.

[Leviticus 22:10a]

34 Whatever remains of the meat of the ordination offering, and of the bread, till morning shall be burned up. They may not be eaten because they are holy.

[Leviticus 8:32]

35 Just as I have told you, so you shall do to Aaron and to his sons. And it will take 7 days to ordain them.

[Leviticus 8:33]

36 Every day present a bull calf as a sin offering by which to take away sins.

[Leviticus 4:3, 14; 8:14; 16:3; 17:11; Hebrews 9:13, 22]

The offering stand is cleansed when you take away sins on it, thus anointing and sanctifying it.

37 It will take 7 days to cleanse and sanctify the offering stand. Afterwards it shall be most holy, and whatever touches it shall be holy.

[Exodus 40:10]

38 Every day present on the offering stand 2 lambs, each a year old.

[Numbers 28:3]

39 Offer the one lamb in the morning, and offer the other lamb between sunset and dusk.

[Numbers 28:4]

40 To go with the 1st lamb, *(its grain offering of)* 1/10th of an ephah of fine flour sprinkled with ¼ of a hin of beaten oil, and its drink offering of ¼ of a hin of wine.

[Numbers 28:5, 7]

41 And to go with the 2nd lamb offered between sunset and dusk, a grain offering and a drink offering like those in the morning, as a sweet-savory roasted offering to Jehovah.

[Numbers 28:8]

42 Offer such burnt offerings constantly throughout your generations at the entrance of the tabernacle, where I will meet with you and speak with you.

[Leviticus 17:3-5]

43 There I will meet with the Israelites, and it will be sanctified by My glory.

44 I will sanctify the tabernacle and the offering stand, as well as Aaron and his sons so they can serve as priests to Me.

45 I will *put My* tabernacle in the midst of the Israelites, and I will be God to them.

[Leviticus 26:11-12; Ezekiel 36:28; 37:27; 2 Corinthians 6:16b]

46 I will put My tabernacle in their midst so they shall know who Jehovah their God is, the One who took them out of Egypt.

[Exodus 3:14; 6:7b; 7:5; 9:16; 10:2; 14:4, 18; 16:2; 29:46; Nehemiah 9:10; Romans 9:17]

CHAPTER 30

1 Make an offering stand for incense of acacia wood.

[Exodus 37:25a]

2 It is to be square, 1.5 feet long, 1.5 feet wide, and 3 feet high. Its horns are to be of one piece with it.

[Exodus 37:25b]

3 Coat it and its horns with pure gold, inside out, and make a gold molding around it.

[Exodus 37:26]

4 Make 2 rings of gold and attach them below its molding on either side, with which to hold the carrying poles.

[Exodus 37:27]

5 And make poles of acacia wood and coat them with gold.

[Exodus 37:28]

6 Put it beyond the curtain, in front of the Box of the Commandments, on which cover I will meet with you.

[Exodus 26:33a; 40:3a, 21a]

7 Every morning Aaron shall burn scented incense on it when he tends the lamps.

[Exodus 40:26-27; 1 Chronicles 6:49; 2 Chronicles 13:11a; Luke 1:8-9]

8 Whenever Aaron lights up the lamps between sunset and dusk, he shall burn incense, a regular incense burning before Jehovah throughout your generations.

9 But, without having been authorized, neither must you burn incense nor must you present a burnt offering or a grain offering or a drink offering.

[Leviticus 10:1-2; Numbers 26:61; 2 Chronicles 26:18-19]

10 And Aaron shall rub blood on all its horns once a year throughout your generations. By the sin offering he takes away the sins from it, and it shall be most holy to Jehovah."

[Exodus 29:36-37; Leviticus 8:15]

11 Jehovah went on to say to Moses:

12 "When you take a census of the Israelites, everyone who was counted shall pay a ransom for his life to Jehovah, so that no plague shall come on them while the census is being taken.

[Numbers 1:2-3; 26:2-4]

13 Everyone who has crossed over to those who were counted shall pay to Jehovah a half shekel according to the standard sanctuary shekel, that is, 20 gerahs to a shekel.

[Exodus 38:26a; Leviticus 27:25; Ezekiel 45:12a]

14 All who have crossed over to those who were counted, from 20 years old and above, shall pay such an amount to Jehovah.

[Exodus 38:26b]

15 In paying the half shekel as ransom for your life to Jehovah, the rich shall not pay more and the poor shall not pay less.

16 Accept from the Israelites the silver as ransom money and use it for the upkeep of the tabernacle, which will remind Jehovah to redeem the lives of the Israelites."

17 Jehovah went on to say to Moses:

18 "Make a washbasin with stand of bronze, and place it between the offering stand *(for burnt offerings)* and the tabernacle, and put water in it.

[Exodus 31:9; 35:16; 38:8; 39:39; 40:30]

19 Aaron and his sons must wash their hands and their feet at it.

[Exodus 29:4; 40:12, 31-32]

20 Before they enter the Most Holy Place to burn incense in the offering stand to Jehovah, they must wash with water, or they shall die.

21 This is a lasting ordinance for them, for him and his descendants throughout their generations: They must wash their hands and their feet that they may not die."

22 Jehovah went on to say to Moses:

23 "As for you, take the best-smelling spices in fluid extract, as follows:

> 500 units *(or 12½ pounds)* of myrrh,
> 250 units *(or 6¼ pounds)* of sweet cinnamon,
> 250 units *(or 6¼ pounds)* of aromatic cane

24 500 units *(or 12½ pounds)* of cassia
and a hin of olive oil

(weighed according to the sanctuary standard)

25 Then blend these into a holy anointing oil, like what an ointment-maker does, and it shall be a holy anointing oil.

[Exodus 31:11; 35:15; 37:29; 39:38]

26 And use it to anoint the following:
[Exodus 40:9a; Leviticus 8:10]

> the tabernacle,
> the Box of the Commandments,

27 the table and all its utensils,
the lampstand and its accessories,
the offering stand for incense,

28 the offering stand for burnt offerings and all its utensils, and the washbasin with stand

29 Sanctify them to make them most holy, and whatever touches them shall be holy.

[Exodus 40:9b]

30 Anoint and sanctify Aaron and his sons so they can serve as priests to Me.

[Exodus 28:41; 30:30; 40:13-15]

31 Say to the Israelites, 'This is to be My holy anointing oil throughout your generations.

32 It must not be applied on human body, and do not make any like it using its composition. It is holy, regard it as holy.

33 Whoever makes an ointment like it, or applies even a small amount of it on a *non-Aaronite*, shall be purged from his people.'"

34 Jehovah went on to say to Moses: "Take the following fragrant spices: stacte, onycha, galbanum, and pure frankincense, in equal amounts.

35 Then blend these into a scented incense, like what a perfumer does, and add salt to keep it pure and clean.

[Exodus 31:11; 35:15; 37:29; 39:38]

36 Crush some of it into fine powder and put some in front of the *(Box of the)* Commandments in the Most Holy Place, where I will meet with you. Regard it as most holy.

37 Do not make incense using the same composition for personal use. Keep it holy for Jehovah.

38 Whoever makes any like it for personal use shall be purged from his people."

CHAPTER 31

1 Jehovah went on to say to Moses:

2 "I picked out Bezalel the son of Uri, son of Hur, of the tribe of Judah,

[Exodus 35:30]

3 and gave him wisdom, insight, and artistic skill in the following:

[Exodus 35:31]

4 in designing and engraving using gold, silver, and bronze;

[Exodus 35:32]

5 in cutting and setting gemstones;

and in carving wood, for him to be able to make every kind of product.

[Exodus 35:33]

6 To work with him, I picked out Oholiab son of Ahisamach, of the tribe of Dan, and everyone whom I have given wisdom, to make all that I have told you, as follows:

[Exodus 35:34-35]

7 the tabernacle and all its furnishings
the Box of the Commandments and its cover

8 the table and all its utensils
the lampstand of pure gold and its accessories
the offering stand for incense

9 the offering stand for burnt offerings and all its utensils
the washbasin with stand

10 the woven garments and the sacred garments
for Aaron the priest and his sons when they serve as priests

11 and the anointing oil and the scented incense
for the Most Holy Place

In accordance with everything that I have told you, so shall they do."

12 Jehovah went on to say to Moses:

13 "Say to the Israelites, 'Above all, observe My sabbath as a symbol between Me and you throughout your generations, for you to know that Jehovah is sanctifying you.

[Exodus 16:23; 31:17a; 34:21b; Leviticus 19:3b, 30a; 26:2a; Ezekiel 20:12, 20]

14 Keep the Sabbath holy. Whoever defiles it shall definitely be put to death. The person who works on that day shall be purged from his people.

[Exodus 20:8; 31:14a; 35:2b; Numbers 15:32-36; Deuteronomy 5:12; Isaiah 56:2; 58:13; Ezekiel 44:24d]

15 Six days you may work, but observe sabbath on the 7th day. It is a day of rest, a holy day to Jehovah. Whoever works on the sabbath day shall definitely be put to death.

[Exodus 20:9-10; 23:12; 34:21; 35:2a; Leviticus 23:3; Deuteronomy 5:13-14]

16 The Israelites must observe sabbath throughout their generations. It is a lasting covenant.

17 It is a lasting symbol between Me and the Israelites, for Jehovah made the heaven and the earth in 6 days, then rested on the 7th day and was refreshed.'"

[Genesis 2:2-3; Exodus 20:11; 31:13; Hebrews 4:4]

18 As soon as God has finished speaking with Moses on Mount Sinai, He gave to him the two stone tablets of Commandments inscribed by His own hand.

[Exodus 24:12; 32:16; 34:1; Deuteronomy 4:13; 5:22; 9:10-11; 10:1-4]

CHAPTER 32

1 Meanwhile, when the people saw that Moses was delaying his coming down from the mountain, they gathered around Aaron and told him: "Get up, make us a god who will lead us. Because as for Moses who led us out of Egypt, we do not know what has happened to him."

[Exodus 32:23; Acts 7:40]

2 Aaron answered them: "Take the gold earrings off the ears of your wives, of your sons, and of your daughters, and bring them to me."

[Exodus 32:24]

3 And all the people took off the gold earrings that they were wearing and brought them to Aaron.

4 He received the gold from them and cast it into an image of a calf with the use of a graving tool.

[Deuteronomy 9:16b; Psalms 106:19a; Acts 7:41a]

And they said: "This is your god, O Israel, who took you out of Egypt!"

[Exodus 32:8b; Nehemiah 9:18; Isaiah 42:17]

5 On seeing this, Aaron made an offering stand in front of it. More so, he made an announcement: "There will be a feast to Jehovah tomorrow."

6 So early in the morning the people presented burnt offerings and fellowship sacrifices. Afterwards they sat down to eat and drink. Then they stood up to have a good time.

[1 Corinthians 10:7]

7 Jehovah then told Moses: "Go down, because the people whom you led out of Egypt have corrupted themselves.

[Deuteronomy 4:16, 25; 9:12a]

8 They have deviated from the way I told them to take.

[Deuteronomy 9:12b, 16c; Judges 2:17b]

They have cast an image of a calf, bowed down to it, and offered sacrifices to it, saying, 'This is your god, O Israel, who took you out of Egypt!'"

[Exodus 32:4b, 6a]

9 Jehovah went on to say to Moses: "I find this people to be stiff-necked *(stubborn)*.

[Exodus 33:3b, 5a; Deuteronomy 9:6b, 13; 31:27; 2 Chronicles 30:8a]

10 So now let me explode My anger against them and annihilate them. Then I will make you into a great nation."

[Genesis 12:2; Exodus 33:5a; Numbers 14:12; Deuteronomy 9:14]

11 Moses tried to calm down Jehovah his God, saying: "O Jehovah, should You explode Your anger against Your people whom You took out of Egypt with great power and a strong hand *('by an Extended Arm and with great plagues' in Exodus 6:6)*.

[Deuteronomy 9:26; Psalms 106:23]

12 Why must the Egyptians say, 'He took them out with an evil motive, to kill them in the mountains and to wipe them off the face of the earth!' --- Turn from Your burning anger and revoke what You have said against Your people.

[Numbers 14:15-16; Deuteronomy 9:28]

13 Remember Abraham, Isaac, and Israel, Your servants to whom You swore by Your name, saying to them, 'I will multiply your offspring as many as the stars in the sky, and I will give to them all the land I have promised on oath as their lasting inheritance."

[Genesis 15:5; 22:17a; 26:4a; Exodus 33:1; Deuteronomy 1:10; 10:22; 1 Chronicles 16:15-18; Nehemiah 9:23; Psalms 105:9-11; Ezekiel 47:14]

14 And Jehovah revoked what He had said He would do to His people.

15 After that Moses left and went down the mountain with the tablets of Commandments in his hands, with inscriptions on either side, back and forth.

16 The tablets were cut out by God and the inscriptions on the tablets were inscribed by God.

[Exodus 24:12; 31:18; 34;1; Deuteronomy 4:13; 5:22; 9:10-11; 10:1-4]

17 Now Joshua heard some noise made by people, so he said to Moses: "There is sound of battle in the camp."

18 He answered: "It doesn't sound a victory song nor a defeat song; I hear a different sound."

19 As soon as Moses got close to the camp and saw the calf and the dancing, he exploded in anger and threw the tablets on impulse, shattering them at the foot of the mountain.

[Deuteronomy 9:17; 10:2]

20 Then he took the calf which the Israelites worshiped and burned it up. Then he pulverized it, scattered it on the face of the water, and made them drink it.

[Deuteronomy 9:21; 2 Chronicles 34:4b, 7a]

21 Afterwards Moses asked Aaron: "What did this people do to you so that you have brought a grave sin on them?"

22 Aaron answered: "My lord, do not explode in anger; you know yourself how bent on evil these people are.

23 They told me, 'Make us a god who will lead us. Because as for Moses who led us out of Egypt, we do not know what has happened to him.'

[Exodus 32:1]

24 Thus I told them, 'Who has any gold, take it off and give it to me.' --- And when I threw the gold into the fire, this calf came out."

[Exodus 32:2]

25 Moses saw through that Aaron condoned the unruly behavior of the people, such a disgrace in the eyes of their opposers.

26 With that Moses stood at the entrance of the camp and said: "Who is on Jehovah's side, come to me!"

And all the Levites gathered to him.

27 Then he said to them: "This is what Jehovah, the God of Israel, says, 'Everyone, strap your sword at your side. Go through the camp from gate to gate and kill your relative, your neighbor, and your friend!'"

[Numbers 25:5; Deuteronomy 13:6-11; 2 Kings 10:25]

28 And the Levites did so, just as Moses had told; and about 3,000 of the people fell that day.

29 Moses went on to say: "Congratulate yourselves today for Jehovah, because He will bestow a blessing on each one of you for going against your son and your brother."

[Numbers 25:10-13]

30 And the very next day Moses said to the people: "Since you have committed a grave sin, I will go up to Jehovah. Perhaps I can ask forgiveness for your sin."

31 Hence Moses went back to Jehovah and said: "This people have committed a grave sin, they have worshiped a god made of gold!"

32 Now, if you will, please forgive their sin; but if not, then erase my name from Your book."

[Psalms 69:28b; Isaiah 4:3; Daniel 12:1c; Luke 10:20; Revelation 3:5]

33 Jehovah answered Moses: "Whoever has sinned against Me I will erase his name from My book.

34 But for now, go, lead the people to where I have told you. My angel will go ahead of you. Now when it's time for Me to punish, I will punish them for their sin."

35 And soon enough Jehovah sent a plague on the people for worshiping the calf which Aaron made.

CHAPTER 33

1 Jehovah went on to say to Moses: "Go, get going, you and the people whom you led out of Egypt, to the land I promised on oath to Abraham, Isaac, and Jacob, saying, 'To your offspring I will give it.'

[Exodus 32:13b; Deuteronomy 34:4a; 1 Chronicles 16:15-18; Psalms 105:9-11]

2 I will send an angel ahead of you to drive out the Canaanites, Amorites, Hittites, Perizzites, Hivites, and Jebusites, **3** from the land overflowing with milk and honey. For I will not go with you because you are a stiff-necked people; I might just annihilate you along the way."

[Exodus 23:23; 32:9-10a; Deuteronomy 9:6, 13-14a; 31:27; 2 Chronicles 30:8a]

4 On hearing such drastic words, the people grieved, and none of them wore jewelries anymore.

5 For *earlier* Jehovah has said to Moses: "Say to the Israelites, 'Since you are a stiff-necked people, if I were to go with you even for a moment I might just annihilate you. Now while I am thinking what to do with you, take off your jewelries.'"

6 And from Mount Horeb *(or Mount Sinai)* onward, the Israelites did not wear jewelries anymore.

7 As for Moses, he pitched his tent far away, outside the camp, and he called it 'Tent of Meeting'. And whoever wanted to consult Jehovah would go to the Tent of Meeting outside the camp.

8 And when Moses went to the Tent, all the people would rise, stand at the entrance of their respective tents, and watch Moses until he entered the Tent.

9 And when Moses entered the Tent, the pillar of cloud would come down and settle at the entrance of the Tent till God had finished speaking with Moses.

[Deuteronomy 31:15]

10 When the people saw the pillar of cloud at the entrance of the Tent, each one would rise and bow down at the entrance of his own tent.

11 And Jehovah spoke with Moses face to face, just as a man would speak with his friend. And when Moses returned to the camp, his assistant, Joshua son of Nun, would remain in the Tent.

[Numbers 12:8; 14:14b; Deuteronomy 34:10]

12 Now Moses said to Jehovah: "You have been telling me, 'Lead this people.' --- What's more, You said, 'I picked you out because you have found favor in My eyes' --- yet You haven't informed me whom You will send with me.

13 If indeed I have found favor in Your eyes, then teach me Your ways so that I may know You *better*, and *thus continue* to find favor in Your eyes. Remember, this nation is Your people."

[Psalms 25:4; 27:11; 86:11; 119:33]

14 He answered: "I will go along and give you peace."

15 He said to Him: "For if You do not go along, then do not take us out of here.

16 For how will it be known that I have found favor in Your eyes, I and Your people, isn't it by Your going along with us, thus making me and Your people distinct from all the rest of the people on the face of the earth?"

17 Jehovah answered Moses: "Ask another thing and I will also do. I picked you out because you have found favor in My eyes."

18 He said: "Please let me see You."

19 He answered: "I will pass by you and confirmed to you that it's Me, Jehovah. I give grace to whomever I find favor, and I show mercy to whomever I take pity."

[Romans 9:15]

20 He went on: "But you may not see My face, for no man may see Me and stay alive."

21 Jehovah went on to say: "There is a rock near Me where you can stand on.

22 As I pass by, I have to put you in a crevice of that rock and cover you with My hand until I have passed by.

23 Afterwards I will remove My hand so you will be able to see My back, but not My face."

CHAPTER 34

1 Then Jehovah told Moses: "Cut out two stones tablets like the first ones, and I will inscribe on them the words that were inscribed on the first tablets, those which you shattered.

[Exodus 24:12; 31:18; 32:16, 19; Deuteronomy 4:13; 5:22; 9:10, 17; 10:1-4]

2 Be ready by morning, for in the morning you must go up to the top of Mount Sinai and there wait for Me.

3 But no one may come up with you and nobody else must be there on the mountain. What's more, no flock or herd should be grazing at the foot of the mountain."

4 Thus Moses cut out two stones tablets like the first ones, and early in the morning went up to Mount Sinai with the two stone tablets in his hands, just as Jehovah has told him.

[Deuteronomy 10:3]

5 And Jehovah came down in a cloud and stood there, confirming it's Him, Jehovah.

[Exodus 33:19a]

6 Then Jehovah passed by in front of him and said: "Jehovah, Jehovah, God merciful and gracious, patient, very loving, and faithful.

[Numbers 14:18a; Nehemiah 9:17b; Psalms 86:15; 103:8; Joel 2:13b; Jonah 4:2b; Nahum 1:3a]

7 He loves thousands, forgives fault, offense, and sin, but exempts no one from punishment. He punishes children and grandchildren, up to the 3rd or 4th generation, for the sins of their parents."

[Exodus 20:5b-6; Numbers 14:18; Deuteronomy 5:9b-10; 7:9-10; Jeremiah 32:18; Nahum 1:3a]

8 And at once Moses bowed down with his face on the ground.

9 Then he said: "O Lord, if indeed I have found favor in Your eyes, please go with us. Although we are a stiff-necked people, you have to forgive our sin and offense and take us as Your *legacy people*.

[Exodus 19:5; Deuteronomy 4:20; 7:6; 9:26, 29; 14:2; 26:18; 32:19; 1 Kings 8:51; Psalms 135:4; 1 Peter 2:9]

10 He answered: "I am going to make a covenant *(with you)*: Before all your people, I will do wonders that have never been thought of anywhere in the whole world or by any nation. All the people among you will see what awe-inspiring action Jehovah will do with you.

11 Your part is to obey what I am telling you, while My part is to drive out from before you the Amorites, the Canaanites, the Hittites, the Perizzites, the Hivites, and the Jebusites.

[Exodus 23:28; 34:24; Deuteronomy 7:1; Psalms 80:8b]

12 Beware not to make a covenant with the inhabitants of the land, to where you are going, or you will be hooked.

[Exodus 23:32; Deuteronomy 7:2c; Judges 2:2a]

13 Instead, pull down their offering stands, shatter their idolatrous posts, and cut down their idolatrous poles.

[Exodus 23:24b; Deuteronomy 7:5; 12:3; Judges 2:2b; 2 Kings 11:18a; 23:14-15; 2 Chronicles 14:3; 31:1a; 34:4a, 7a]

14 Do not bow down to any other god, because Jehovah, whose name means Jealous, is a jealous God.

[Exodus 20:5a; 22:20; 23:13, 24a; Deuteronomy 4:24b; 5:9a; 6:14-15; 11:16-17; 29:26-27; 30:17-18; 32:21; Joshua 23:7b; 24:19a; 2 Kings 17:35; 2 Chronicles 7:19-20; Psalms 81:9; Isaiah 2:8-9; 46:6-7; Jeremiah 1:16; 16:10-11; 22:8-9; 25:6; Ezekiel 5:13; 39:25; Daniel 3:28; Nahum 1:2a]

15 For when you make a covenant with the inhabitants of the land, who worship their gods and offer sacrifices to them, they will surely invite you to eat of their sacrifices.

[Numbers 25:1-2; Acts 15:29; 21:25; 1 Corinthians 10:19-20]

16 Then you will let your sons marry their daughters, and their daughters will make your sons worship their gods the way they do.

[Deuteronomy 7:3-4; Judges 3:6; 1 Kings 11:1-2; Ezra 9:2; Nehemiah 13:25-26]

17 Do not worship carved images.

[Exodus 20:4; 34:17; Leviticus 19:4; 26:1; Deuteronomy 4:15-19, 23b, 25; 5:8; 9:12, 16; 16:21-22; 27:15; 1 Kings 14:9; 2 Kings 17:12, 41; Psalms 78:58; 97:7; 106:19-20; 115:4-8; 135:15-18; Isaiah 40:19-20; 41:29; 42:8, 17; 44:9-20; 45:20; Jeremiah 2:27-28; 10:3-5, 14-15; 51:17-18; Hosea 13:2; Micah 1:7a; 5:13-14; Nahum 1:14; Habakkuk 2:18-19; Acts 17:29-30; Revelation 9:20]

18 *First,* commemorate the Feast of Unleavened Bread.

[Exodus 12:17; 23:15; Leviticus 23:6a; Deuteronomy 16:16; 2 Chronicles 8:13; 30:21; 35:17; Ezra 6:22a; Ezekiel 45:21b; Luke 22:1; Acts 12:3b; 1 Corinthians 5:8]

Just as I have told you, eat unleavened bread 7 days at the scheduled time and date in the month of Abib, on which month you came out of Egypt.

[Exodus 12:18; 23:15b; Leviticus 23:6; Numbers 28:17a]

19 Every male that opens the womb is Mine. As for your livestock, the firstling of cattle and of sheep.

[Genesis 4:4; Exodus 13:2, 12; 22:29b; Numbers 18:15a; Deuteronomy 15:19; Nehemiah 10:36; Luke 2:23]

20 Redeem the firstling of your donkey with a lamb. If you will not, then break its neck. More so, redeem every firstborn son of yours. They must not appear before Me empty-handed.

[Exodus 13:13, 15b; 23:15c; Numbers 18:15b]

21 Six days you may work, but observe sabbath on the 7th day. Observe sabbath even in times of plowing or harvesting.

[Exodus 16:23; 20:9-10; 23:12; 31:13a, 15-16; 35:2a; Leviticus 19:3b, 30a; 23:3; 26:2a; Deuteronomy 5:13-15]

22 *Second, commemorate* the Festival of Weeks *(Feast of Harvest in Exodus 23:16a, while Festival of Pentecost in Acts 2:1)* with the first ripe fruits of your wheat harvest.

[Numbers 28:26; Deuteronomy 16:10; 2 Chronicles 8:13b]

And *third, commemorate* the Feast of Ingathering *(Festival of Booths in Leviticus 23:16b, Deuteronomy 16:13, 2 Chronicles 8:13, Ezra 3:4, Nehemiah 8:14 & Zechariah 14:16, while Festival of Tabernacles in John 7:2)* at the end of the year.

[Leviticus 23:16b]

23 Three times a year all men of yours shall appear before *Me*, the God of Israel.

[Exodus 23:14, 17; Deuteronomy 16:16; 2 Chronicles 8:13]

24 When you go to meet with Jehovah your God 3 times a year, I will drive out the nations from before you and expand your territory, and nobody can grab your land.

[Exodus 34:11)

25 You must not eat the meat of My Passover sacrifice along with anything made with yeast. Do not leave any of it till morning.

[Exodus 12:8, 10a; 23:18; Leviticus 7:15; 22:30; Numbers 9:11b-12a; Deuteronomy 16:3-4]

26 Bring the best of the first ripe fruits of your soil to the temple of Jehovah your God.

[Exodus 23:19a; Leviticus 2:12; 23:10; Deuteronomy 26:2; Nehemiah 10:35; Proverbs 3:9; Ezekiel 44:30]

You must not boil a baby goat in the milk of its mother.

[Exodus 23:19b; Deuteronomy 14:21d]

27 Jehovah went on to say to Moses: "Copy the commandments on which I based the covenant I make with you."

[Exodus 24:4a; Deuteronomy 27:8]

28 And as he was copying the words of the covenant, that is, the 10 Commandments, he was there with Jehovah 40 days and 40 nights without eating and drinking.

[Exodus 24:4a, 18]

29 When Moses went down from Mount Sinai with the two tablets of Commandments in his hand, he was not aware that his face was radiant for having spoken with Him.

30 On seeing the radiant face of Moses, Aaron and all the Israelites were afraid to come near to him.

[2 Corinthians 3:7b]

31 But when Moses called them and talk to them, Aaron and all the chieftains of the community came near to him.

32 And when all the Israelites came near to him, he relayed to them all that Jehovah had spoken with him on Mount Sinai.

33 When Moses has finished speaking with them, he put a veil over his face.

[2 Corinthians 3:13]

34 But when Moses went in before Jehovah to speak with Him, he did not wear a veil until he came out. Then Moses relayed to the Israelites what he has been told.

35 Again, when the Israelites saw his radiant face, Moses wore a veil over his face until such time he went in to speak with Him.

CHAPTER 35

1 Sometime later Moses gathered the whole Israelite community and said to them: "Jehovah commands you to do the following:

2 Six days you may work, but keep the 7th day holy. It is a sabbath, a day of rest to Jehovah. Whoever works on that day shall be put to death.

[Exodus 20:9-10; 23:12; 31:14b-15a; 34:21a; Leviticus 23:3; Numbers 15:32-36; Deuteronomy 5:13-14]

3 You must not light a fire anywhere in your house on the sabbath day."

4 Moses went on to say to the whole Israelite community: "Jehovah gave the following commands:

5 Everyone among you who is willing to give may bring an offering to Jehovah, such as follows:

   gold, silver, and bronze **[Exodus 25:3]**

6 blue, purple and red yarns, fine linen, and goat hair
[Exodus 25:4]

7 tanned sheepskins, seal fur, and acacia wood **[Exodus 25:5]**

8 oil for light, and spice extracts for the anointing oil and for the scented incense **[Exodus 25:6]**

9 onyx stones and gemstones to be set on the ephod and on the breastplate **[Exodus 25:7]**

10 And all the skilled ones among you may come and make all that Jehovah has told, as follows:

11 the wall tents and the roof tents of the tabernacle **[Exodus 26:7, 14]**

    their hooks, panel frames, crossbars, posts, and baseplates **[Exodus 26:6, 11, 15-17, 19, 21, 25-27]**

12 the Box, its poles, its cover **[Exodus 25:10, 13, 17]**
    and the curtain to screen it off **[Exodus 26:31]**

13 the table, its poles, all its utensils **[Exodus 25:23, 28-29]**
    and the showbread **[Exodus 25:30]**

14 the lampstand and its accessories, its lamps **[Exodus 25:31-38]**

    and the oil for light **[Exodus 25:6a]**

15 the offering stand for incense and its carrying poles **[Exodus 30:1, 5]**

    the anointing oil and the scented incense **[Exodus 25:6b]**

    and the curtain for the entrance of the tabernacle **[Exodus 26:36]**

16 the offering stand for burnt offerings **[Exodus 27:1]**
    its bronze grill, its poles, all its utensils **[Exodus 27:3-4, 6]**

and the washbasin with stand **[Exodus 30:18a]**

17 the wall tents enclosing the courtyard **[Exodus 27:9]**

their posts and baseplates
[Exodus 27:10a, 11b, 12b, 14b, 15b, 16b, 18b]

and the curtain for the entrance of the courtyard
[Exodus 27:16]

18 the tent pins and cords of the tabernacle and of the courtyard **[Exodus 27:19]**

19 the woven garments to be worn when burning incense in the Most Holy Place, and the sacred garments for Aaron and his sons when they serve as priests." **[Exodus 28:4]**

20 Hence the whole Israelite community left the presence of Moses.

21 Then they came back, everyone who is willing to give, and brought an offering to Jehovah for the construction of the tabernacle, for any use, and for the sacred garments.

22 And they kept coming, men as well as women, everyone who is willing to give. They brought brooches, earrings, rings, female jewelries, all kinds of gold articles, and presented these gold as a wave offering to Jehovah.

23 And those who have blue, purple, and red yarns, fine linen and goat hair, and tanned sheepskins and seal fur, brought them.

24 All those who have silver and bronze brought them as an offering to Jehovah, and all those who have acacia wood brought it for any use.

25 All the women skilled in spinning brought blue, purple, and red fine linen yarns and spun them.

26 And all the other skilled women spun the goat hair.

27 The chieftains brought onyx stones and gemstones to be set on the ephod and on the breastplate, **28** oil for light, and spice extracts for the anointing oil and for the scented incense.

29 Every Israelite man and woman who was willing to give brought a freewill offering to Jehovah for any use, for all the work which Jehovah had told them to do through Moses.

30 Then Moses said to the Israelites: "Jehovah has picked out Bezalel (the son of Uri, son of Hur), of the tribe of Judah,

[Exodus 31:2]

31 and He has given him wisdom, insight, and artistic skill in the following: **[Exodus 31:3]**

32 in designing and engraving using gold, silver, and bronze; **[Exodus 31:4]**

33 in cutting and setting gemstones;

and in carving wood, to be able to make every kind of ingenious product. **[Exodus 31:5]**

34 And He has put in his heart to teach Oholiab son of Ahisamach, of the tribe of Dan.

[Exodus 31:6a]

35 He has given them wisdom so they can do the work of an artist, an embroiderer, and a loom weaver who weaves in blue, purple, and red fine linen yarns, men who can design and make every kind of artwork."

[Exodus 31:6b]

CHAPTER 36

1 Bezalel will work with Oholiab and with all the other skilled ones, to whom Jehovah has given wisdom and skill so that they can do all the work for the holy project in accordance with His instructions.

[Exodus 31:2-6; 35:30-35; 38:22-23]

2 Hence Moses called Bezalel, Oholiab, and all the skilled ones whom Jehovah had given wisdom, everyone who knew how to do the work.

3 And they received from Moses all the offerings that the Israelites have brought for the holy project so that they can start working. Aside from that, they *(the Israelites)* would bring to him a freewill offering every morning.

4 Before long all the skilled ones, who were working for the holy project, came one by one, **5** and said to Moses: "The people are bringing much more than what is needed for the work that Jehovah has told to be done."

6 With that Moses told them to circulate an announcement throughout the camp, saying: "Men and women, do not bring anymore raw materials for the holy project."

And the people stopped bringing more, **7** for indeed the raw materials were more than enough to finish the whole project.

8 So the most skilled ones started weaving ten wall tents for the tabernacle using blue, purple and red linen twisted yarns, and embroidered cherubs on them.

[Exodus 26:1]

9 All the wall tents have the same measure --- 42 feet long and 6 feet high.

[Exodus 26:2]

10 They joined the 5 wall tents into one set, and the other 5 wall tents into another set.

[Exodus 26:3]

11 Afterwards they made loops of blue yarn along the edge of the end wall tent in the one set and did the same in the other set.

[Exodus 26:4]

12 They made 50 loops on the end wall tent in the one set, and another 50 loops in the other set.

[Exodus 26:5]

13 Finally they cast 50 hooks of gold with which they coupled the *(2 sets of)* wall tents into one tabernacle.

[Exodus 26:6]

14 They went on to make eleven roof tents of goat hair for the tabernacle.

[Exodus 26:7]

15 All the roof tents have the same measure --- 45 feet long by 6 feet wide.

[Exodus 26:8]

16 Then they joined the 5 roof tents into one set and the other 6 roof tents into another set.

[Exodus 26:9a]

17 Next he made 50 loops along the edge of the end roof tent in the one set and another 50 loops in the other set.

[Exodus 26:10]

18 Afterwards he cast 50 hooks of bronze with which to couple the *(2 sets of)* roof tents into one roof.

[Exodus 26:11]

19 And he made an inner roof top tent of tanned sheepskins and an outer roof top tent of seal fur for the tabernacle.

[Exodus 26:14]

20 Then he made upright panel frames of acacia wood for the tabernacle.

[Exodus 26:15]

21 Each panel frame was 15 feet long by 2.25 feet wide.

[Exodus 26:16]

22 Each panel frame has 2 fitting tenons. That was how he made all the panel frames of the tabernacle.

[Exodus 26:17]

23 He made 20 panel frames for the south side of the tabernacle.

[Exodus 26:18]

24 And he made 40 silver baseplates to go under the 20 panel frames --- 2 baseplates under each panel frame that has 2 fitting tenons.

[Exodus 26:19]

25 He made 20 panel frames for the north side of the tabernacle, **26** and their 40 silver baseplates --- 2 baseplates under each panel frame.

[Exodus 26:20-21]

27 He made 6 panel frames for the west side, at the back of the tabernacle.

[Exodus 26:22]

28 He made 2 panel frames as corner connectors for the 2 corners at the back of the tabernacle.

[Exodus 26:23]

29 The 2 corner connectors were coupled at the top and at the bottom with a single ring each.

[Exodus 26:24]

30 In all, 8 panel frames and 16 silver baseplates *(for the west side)* --- 2 baseplates under each panel frame.

[Exodus 26:25]

31 He went on to make 5 crossbars of acacia wood for the panel frames on the one *(south)* side of the tabernacle, **32** another 5 crossbars for the panel frames on the other *(north)* side of the tabernacle, and another 5 crossbars for the panel frames for the 2 corners at the back *(or west side)* of the tabernacle .

[Exodus 26:26-27]

33 He made the middle crossbar to run from end to end at the center of the panel frames.

[Exodus 26:28]

34 He coated the panel frames and crossbars with gold, and cast rings of gold to hold the crossbars.

[Exodus 26:29]

35 He made a curtain of blue, purple, and red fine linen yarns, and embroidered cherubs on it.

[Exodus 26:31]

36 For it, he made 4 posts of acacia and coated them with gold, and cast 4 baseplates of silver for them; their hooks were of gold.

[Exodus 26:32-33a]

37 He wove a curtain in blue, purple and red linen twisted yarns for the entrance of the tabernacle.

[Exodus 26:36]

38 Then he coated their 5 posts with gold, but their 5 baseplates were of bronze; their hooks and fasteners were of gold.

[Exodus 26:37]

CHAPTER 37

1 Then Bezalel made a Box of acacia wood, 3.75 feet long, 2.25 feet wide, and 2.25 feet high.

[Exodus 25:10]

2 He coated it with pure gold, inside out, and made a gold molding around it.

 [Exodus 25:11]

3 Afterwards he cast 4 rings of gold and attached them above its 4 feet, with 2 rings on either side.

[Exodus 25:12]

4 Next he made poles of acacia wood and coated them with gold.

[Exodus 25:13]

5 He inserted the poles into the rings on either side of the Box with which to carry it.

[Exodus 25:14]

6 He went on to make a cover of pure gold, 3.75 feet long and 2.25 feet wide.

[Exodus 25:17]

7 He also made two cherubs of hammered gold and placed them on the ends of the cover, **8** that is, the one cherub on the one end and the other cherub on the other end.

[Exodus 25:18-19]

9 The two wings of each cherub were spread forward to screen off the cover, with the cherubs facing each other and their eyes toward the cover.

[Exodus 25:20]

10 He made a table of acacia wood, 3 feet long, 1.5 feet wide, and 2.25 feet high.

[Exodus 25:23]

11 Then he coated it with pure gold and made a gold molding around it.

[Exodus 25:24]

12 Next he made a rim around it, the span of a hand, and made a gold molding around the rim.

[Exodus 25:25]

13 More so, he cast 4 rings of gold and attached them to the 4 corners above its 4 feet.

[Exodus 25:26]

14 The rings are put close to the rim of the table to hold the carrying poles.

[Exodus 25:27]

15 Then he made poles of acacia wood with which to carry the table, and coated them with gold.

[Exodus 25:28]

16 Afterwards he made utensils to be placed on the table --- plates, cups, bowls, and pitchers, all of pure gold.

[Exodus 25:29]

17 He made a lampstand of hammered pure gold. Its base and *decorative* branches, calyxes, and flower knobs were of one piece with it.

[Exodus 25:31]

18 Six branches extended from either side of the lampstand: 3 branches from one side and 3 branches from the other side.

[Exodus 25:32]

19 Three cups shaped like almond flowers were on every branch on the one side, and under every cup their flower knobs. Likewise, 3 cups shaped like almond flowers were on every branch on the other side, and under every cup their flower knobs. That is how it was for the 6 branches extending from the lampstand.

[Exodus 25:33]

20 But on the lampstand shaft there were 4 cups shaped like almond flowers, and under every cup their flower knobs.

[Exodus 25:34]

21 Two flower knobs were under every cup on the one side, and 2 flower knobs under every cup on the other side. That is how it was for the 6 branches extending from the lampstand.

[Exodus 25:35]

22 The flower knobs and the branches extending from the lampstand were of one piece with it, all of hammered pure gold.

[Exodus 25:36]

23 Then he made its 7 lamps, wick trimmers, and fire holders of pure gold.

[Exodus 25:37-38]

24 He used one talent *(or 75 pounds)* of pure gold in making it and all its accessories.

[Exodus 25:39]

25 Next he made an offering stand for incense of acacia wood, with 4 horns of one piece with it. It is square, 1.5 feet long, 1.5 feet wide, and 3 feet high.

[Exodus 30:1-2]

26 Then he coated it and its horns with pure gold, inside out. Then he made a gold molding around it.

[Exodus 30:3]

27 He cast 2 rings of gold below the gold molding and attached them on either side to hold the carrying poles.

[Exodus 30:4]

28 Then he made poles of acacia wood and coated them with gold.

[Exodus 30:5]

29 Finally, he blended the holy anointing oil, like what an ointment maker does, and the pure scented incense *(like what a perfumer does)*.

[Exodus 30:23-25, 34-35]

CHAPTER 38

1 He went on to make an offering stand of acacia wood for burnt offerings. It was square, 7.5 feet long, 7.5 feet wide, and 4.5 feet high.

[Exodus 27:1]

2 He made horns on its 4 corners, of one piece with it, and coated them with bronze.

[Exodus 27:2]

3 Then he made utensils for the offering stand --- ash buckets, shovels, basins, forks, and fire holders, all of bronze.

[Exodus 27:3]

4 He also made a grill of bronze, net design pattern, and installed it at the center, under the ledge.

[Exodus 27:4]

5 Next he cast 4 rings and attached them to the 4 corners of the bronze grill to hold the carrying poles.

[Exodus 27:5]

6 After that he made poles of acacia wood and coated them with bronze.

[Exodus 27:6]

7 Then he inserted the carrying poles of hollow planks into the rings on either side of the offering stand.

[Exodus 27:7-8]

8 Then he made a washbasin with stand of bronze, which bronze were taken from the mirrors of the women serving at the entrance of the tabernacle.

[Exodus 30:18a]

9 Then he made *wall tents for* the courtyard.

For the south side of the courtyard, the wall tents were of fine twisted linen, 150 feet long.

[Exodus 27:9]

10 Their 20 posts and 20 baseplates were of bronze. The posts' hooks and fasteners were of silver.

[Exodus 27:10]

11 For the north side, *(the wall tents were)* 150 feet long. Their 20 posts and 20 baseplates were of bronze. The posts' hooks and fasteners were of silver.

[Exodus 27:11]

12 But for the west side, the wall tents were 75 feet long. Their posts 10 and their baseplates 10. The posts' hooks and fasteners were of silver.

[Exodus 27:12]

13 For the east side, *(the wall tents were)* 75 feet long.

[Exodus 27:13]

14 For the one side of the entrance, the wall tents were 22.5 feet *long*. Their posts 3 and their baseplates 3.

[Exodus 27:14]

15 And so for the other side of the entrance of the courtyard, the wall tents were 22.5 feet *long*. Their posts 3 and their baseplates 3.

[Exodus 27:15]

16 The wall tents enclosing the courtyard were all of fine twisted linen.

17 The baseplates of the posts were of bronze. The hooks and fasteners of all the posts of the courtyard were of silver.

[Exodus 27:17]

18 The curtain for the entrance of the courtyard was woven in blue, purple, and red fine twisted linen. It was 30 feet long and 7.5 feet high, the same *(height)* as the wall tents of the courtyard.

[Exodus 27:16a]

19 Its 4 posts and 4 baseplates were of bronze. Their hooks and fasteners were of silver.

[Exodus 27:16b]

20 All the tent pins of the tabernacle and of the courtyard all around were of bronze.

[Exodus 27:19]

21 This is the inventory for the tabernacle, that is, the Tabernacle of the Commandments, inventoried at the command of Moses, and done by the Levites under the supervision of Ithamar son of Aaron the priest.

22 And Bezalel (the son of Uri, son of Hur) of the tribe of Judah, did all that Jehovah had told Moses.

[Exodus 31:2-5]

23 With him was Oholiab son of Ahisamach, of the tribe of Dan, an artist, an embroiderer, and a loom weaver who weaves in blue, purple and red fine linen yarns.

[Exodus 31:6]

24 All the gold from the wave offering, for any use in the holy project, weighed 29 talents of gold and 730 shekels *(or a sum of 2,193 pounds)*, according to the standard sanctuary shekel.

25 And the silver paid by those who were counted among the community weighed 100 talents and 1,775 shekels *(or a sum of 7,545 pounds)* according to the standard sanctuary shekel.

26 Everyone who had crossed over to those who were counted, from 20 years old and above, a total of 603,550 men, paid a half shekel *(or 1 beka)* according to the sanctuary shekel.

[Exodus 30:13-14]

27 One hundred talents *(or 7,500 pounds)* of silver were used in casting 100 baseplates for the tabernacle curtains; 100 talents *(or 75 pounds of silver)* for 100 baseplates; 1 talent per baseplate.

28 With the remaining 1,775 shekels *(or 45 pounds of silver)*, he made silver-plated hooks and fasteners for the posts.

29 And the bronze from the wave offering weighed 70 talents and 2,400 shekels *(or a total of 5,310 pounds)*, **30** which he made into baseplates for the curtain of the tabernacle, the bronze-coated offering stand, its bronze grill and utensils, **31** the baseplates for the wall tents all around, the baseplates for the curtain of the courtyard entrance, and all the tent pins of the tabernacle and of the courtyard all around.

CHAPTER 39

1 And they wove garments in blue, purple and red yarns to be worn when burning incense in the Most Holy Place, and made sacred garments for Aaron, just as Jehovah had told Moses.

2 They wove an ephod in gold, blue, purple and red linen twisted yarns.

[Exodus 28:6]

3 They hammered out gold sheets, cut them into thin strips, and wove them in blue, purple and red fine linen *yarns*.

[Exodus 28:5]

4 For it, they made (2) shoulder straps that can be tied up.

[Exodus 28:7]

5 And the sash, for holding up, was made of the same material --- of gold, blue, purple and red fine twisted linen, just as Jehovah had told Moses.

[Exodus 28:8]

6 Then they mounted the onyx stones in filigree settings, on which the names of Israel's sons were engraved like a seal.

[Exodus 28:9-11]

7 They fastened them *(the onyx stones)* on the ephod's shoulder straps as stones to be reminded of Israel's sons, just as Jehovah had told Moses.

[Exodus 28:12]

8 Then they wove a breastplate in gold, blue, purple and red fine twisted linen.

[Exodus 28:15]

9 The breastplate was square when folded, and when folded its length and width   like the span of a hand.

[Exodus 28:16]

10 Then they mounted 4 rows of gemstones on it, as follows:

   The 1st row was of ruby, topaz, and emerald.

[Exodus 28:17]

11 The 2nd row was of turquoise, sapphire, and jasper.

[Exodus 28:18]

12 The 3rd row was of leshem, agate, and amethyst.

[Exodus 28:19]

13 And the 4th row was of chrysolite, onyx, and jade.

   These were mounted in gold filigree settings.

[Exodus 28:20]

14 And they engraved on the stones the names of Israel's 12 sons, like a seal, representing the 12 tribes.

[Exodus 28:21]

15 They encircled the breastplate with ropelike chains of pure gold.

[Exodus 28:22]

16 Then they made 2 gold filigree settings and 2 rings of gold, and attached the rings to the 2 *upper* ends of the breastplate.

[Exodus 28:23]

17 Afterwards they inserted in layer the 2 gold ropelike chains into the 2 gold rings at the *upper* ends of the breastplate.

[Exodus 28:24]

18 And they tied the ends of the 2 ropelike chains to the 2 filigree settings that are attached to the ephod's shoulder straps at the front.

[Exodus 28:25]

19 Next they made 2 rings of gold and attached them to the 2 *lower* ends of the breastplate, to be tucked in beneath the ephod.

[Exodus 28:26]

20 Then they made 2 rings of gold and attached them to the shoulder straps of the ephod from below, at the front near the seam, above the sash of the ephod.

[Exodus 28:27]

21 Finally, to hold up the breastplate above the sash of the ephod and not come loose atop the ephod, they tied the breastplate to the ephod by their rings with a blue ribbon, just as Jehovah had told Moses.

[Exodus 28:28]

22 Then they wove the sleeveless robe of the ephod in all blue yarn.

[Exodus 28:31]

23 And to keep the neck hole of the sleeveless robe from tearing, a collar was put around it, like the collar of a scale armor.

[Exodus 28:32]

24 Then they sewed pomegranates of blue, purple and red twisted yarns on the hem of the sleeveless robe.

[Exodus 28:33a]

25 More so, they also made bells of pure gold and placed them between the pomegranates all around the hem of the sleeveless robe, **26** that is, a bell and a pomegranate alternating on the hem of the sleeveless robe, *to be worn when burning incense,* just as Jehovah had told Moses.

[Exodus 28:33b-35]

27 Next the wove *checkered* coats of fine linen for Aaron and his sons, **28** as well as turbans of fine linen, *bonnets* of fine linen, shorts of linen twisted yarns, **29** and sashes woven in blue, purple and red linen twisted yarns, just as Jehovah had told Moses.

[Exodus 28:39, 42]

30 Finally they made a shiny plate of pure gold, the label of holiness, and engraved on it 'JEHOVAH IS HOLY' like a seal.

[Exodus 28:36]

31 Then they tied it to the front of the turban with a blue ribbon, just as Jehovah had told Moses.

[Exodus. 28:37]

32 Thus all the work for the tabernacle was completed. The Israelites did so in accordance with all that Jehovah had told Moses. They did exactly.

33 And they brought the tabernacle to Moses ---
　its furnishings, its wall tents, its hooks,
　its panel frames, its crossbars,
　its posts, and its baseplates;

34 its inner roof top tent of tanned sheepskins,

its outer roof top tent of seal fur,
and the curtain to screen it off;

35 the Box of the Commandments,
its poles and cover;

36 the table, its utensils, and the showbread;

37 the lampstand of pure gold, its rows of lamps,
all its accessories, and the oil for light;

38 the gold-coated offering stand,
the anointing oil, the scented incense,
and the curtain for the entrance of the Most Holy Place;

39 the bronze-coated offering stand,
its grill of bronze, its poles, all its utensils,
and the washbasin with stand;

40 the wall tents enclosing the courtyard,
their posts, their baseplates,
the curtain for the entrance of the courtyard,
its tent cords, its tent pins,
and all the accessories of the tabernacle;

41 the woven garments to be worn
when burning incense in the Most Holy Place,
and the sacred garments for Aaron the priest
and his sons when they serve as priests.

42 Just as Jehovah had instructed Moses, so the Israelites did all the work.

43 When Moses inspected all the work, it was done just as Jehovah had instructed. Hence Moses blessed them.

CHAPTER 40

1 Then Jehovah told Moses:

2 "On the 1st day of the 1st month, set up the Most Holy Place of the tabernacle.

[Exodus 40:17]

3 Put the Commandments in the Box, and shut off accessibility to the Box with the curtain.

[Exodus 40:20-21]

4 Bring the table in and arrange what should be on it. Bring in also the lampstand and lit up its lamps.

[Exodus 40:22-25]

5 Place the gold-coated offering stand for incense in front of the Box of the Commandments, and hang the curtain at the entrance.

[Exodus 40:26-28]

6 Place the offering stand for burnt offerings in front of the entrance of the tabernacle.

[Exodus 40:29]

7 Place the washbasin between the offering stand *(for burnt offerings)* and the tabernacle, and put water in it.

[Exodus 40:30]

8 Install the wall tents around the courtyard, and hang the curtain at the entrance of the courtyard.

[Exodus 40:33]

9 Anoint the tabernacle and all that is in it with the anointing oil. Thus you sanctify it and all its furnishings, and it shall be holy.

[Exodus 30:26-28]

10 Anoint the offering stand for burnt offerings and all its utensils. Thus you sanctify the offering stand, and it shall be most holy.

[Exodus 30:28a]

11 Anoint and sanctify also the washbasin with stand.

[Exodus 30:28b]

12 Afterwards present Aaron and his sons at the entrance of the tabernacle, and wash them with water.

[Exodus 40:31-32]

13 Put the sacred garments on Aaron, anoint him, and sanctify him so he can serve as priest to Me.

[Exodus 28:41; 30:30]

14 Afterwards present his sons and put the robes on them.

[Exodus 28:41a; 30:30]

15 Anoint them just as you have anointed their father so they can serve as priests to Me. Their anointing shall qualify them to serve as priests as long as they live."

[Exodus 28:41b; 29:9b]

16 And Moses did in accordance with all that Jehovah had told him; he did exactly.

17 Thus on the 1st day of the 1st month of the 2nd year the tabernacle was set up.

[Exodus 40:2]

18 In setting up the tabernacle, Moses put the baseplates in place, set up the panel frames, and installed the crossbars.

19 Then Moses spread the roof tents over the tabernacle and placed the roof top tents on top, just as Jehovah had told him.

[Exodus 36:14, 19]

20 Afterwards he put the Commandments in the Box, inserted the poles into the rings of the Box, and put its cover.

[Exodus 25:14-16, 21]

21 Then Moses brought the Box of the Commandments into the Most Holy Place, and hung the curtain to shut off accessibility to the Box, just as Jehovah had told him.

[Exodus 40:3]

22 Next he placed the table in the Holy Place, on the north side of the tabernacle, outside the curtain.

[Exodus 40:4a]

23 Then Moses arranged (2) rows of bread on it before Jehovah, just as Jehovah had told him.

[Exodus 40:4a]

24 After that he placed the lampstand in the Holy Place, opposite the table, on the south side of the tabernacle.

[Exodus 40:4b]

25 Then Moses lit up the lamps before Jehovah, just as Jehovah had told him.

[Exodus 40:4b]

26 Next Moses placed the gold-coated offering stand in the Most Holy Place, beyond the curtain, **27** on which scented incense is to be burned, just as Jehovah had told him.

[Exodus 40:5a]

28 Finally he hung the curtain at the entrance of the tabernacle.

[Exodus 40:5b]

29 And Moses placed the offering stand for burnt offerings in front of the entrance of the tabernacle, on which burnt offerings and grain offerings are to be offered, just as Jehovah had told him.

[Exodus 40:6]

30 Then he placed the washbasin between the offering stand *(for burnt offerings)* and the tabernacle, and put water in it for washing.

[Exodus 40:7]

31 And Moses, Aaron, and his sons washed their hands and their feet at it.

[Exodus 30:19]

32 They would wash whenever they enter the Most Holy Place to burn incense, just as Jehovah had told Moses.

[Exodus 30:20]

33 Finally he set up the wall tents enclosing the tabernacle and the offering stand, and hung the curtain at the entrance of the courtyard.

[Exodus 40:8]

Thus Moses has finished the work.

34 And the cloud covered the tabernacle, and the glory of Jehovah filled the Most Holy Place.

[Numbers 9:15]

35 Moses could not enter the tabernacle because the cloud settled above it and the glory of Jehovah filled the Most Holy Place.

[2 Chronicles 7:2; Revelation 15:8a]

36 Now in all their journeys, when the cloud moved away from the tabernacle, the Israelites would break camp.

[Numbers 9:17]

37 But if the cloud did not move away, they would not break camp until the day it moved away.

[Numbers 9:18b-22]

38 During all their journeys, the cloud of Jehovah shaded the tabernacle by day, and the fire glowed in it by night, in the sight of all the house of Israel.

[Numbers 9:15-16]

Understanding
LEVITICUS
Independent of
Earthly Religions

DEDICATION

I dedicate this book
to every human who is sickly,
either because of faithlessness
or
because of sinfulness

TABLE OF CONTENTS

CHAPTER 1

CHAPTER 2

CHAPTER 3

CHAPTER 4

CHAPTER 5

CHAPTER 6

CHAPTER 7

CHAPTER 8

CHAPTER 9

CHAPTER 10

CHAPTER 11

CHAPTER 12

CHAPTER 13

CHAPTER 14

CHAPTER 15

CHAPTER 16

CHAPTER 17

CHAPTER 18

CHAPTER 19

CHAPTER 20

CHAPTER 21

CHAPTER 22

CHAPTER 23

CHAPTER 24

CHAPTER 25

CHAPTER 26

CHAPTER 27

CHAPTER 1

1 From the Most Holy Place Jehovah called Moses and told him:

2 "Say to the Israelites, 'When anyone of you offers an animal sacrifice to Jehovah, it shall either be from the herd or from the flock.

[Leviticus 22:19-21; Deuteronomy 16:2]

3 If his burnt offering is from the herd, it should be a male *(bull)* without defect. He shall present it of his own accord before Jehovah at the entrance of the tabernacle.

[Exodus 29:10a; Leviticus 4:4a, 14; 16:3; 17:3-4; Deuteronomy 15:21; 17:1; Malachi 1:13]

4 He shall lay his hand on the head of his burnt offering, and it will be graciously accepted from him by which to take away his sin.

[Exodus 29:10b; Leviticus 4:4b, 15a; 8:14]

5 Then the bull shall be slaughtered before Jehovah at the entrance of the tabernacle, and Aaron's sons the priests shall spatter its blood all over the offering stand.

[Exodus 29:11; Leviticus 4:4; 17:3-6a]

6 The burnt offering shall be deskinned and cut into parts.

[Exodus 29:17a]

7 Aaron's sons the priests shall arrange firewood on the offering stand.

8 Aaron's sons the priests shall match up the parts to one another up to the head, and put them, along with all the fat, over the firewood on the offering stand.

[Exodus 29:17; Leviticus 1:12, 17; 6:12; 8:20; 9:13]

9 Then the entrails and legs will be washed with water, and the *(officiating)* priest shall roast them altogether on the offering stand for burnt offerings as a sweet-savory roasted offering to Jehovah.

[Genesis 8:21; Ephesians 5:2b; Philippians 4:18b]

10 If his burnt offering is from the flock, it should either be a male lamb or a kid goat, without defect.

[Leviticus 22:19-21; Malachi 1:13; 1 Peter 1:18-19]

11 It shall be slaughtered at the north side of the offering stand before Jehovah, and Aaron's sons the priests shall spatter its blood all over the offering stand.

[Exodus 29:16; Leviticus 3:8, 13]

12 The priest shall cut it into parts and match the parts to one another up to the head, and put them, along with all the fat, over the firewood on the offering stand.

[Exodus 29:17; Leviticus 6:12; 8:20; 9:13]

13 Then the entrails and legs will be washed with water, and the priest shall roast them altogether on the offering stand for burnt offerings as a sweet-savory roasted offering to Jehovah.

[Genesis 8:21; Exodus 12:9; 29:17b-18; Leviticus 8:21; Ephesians 5:2b; Philippians 4:18b]

14 If his burnt offering to Jehovah is from the birds, it should either be turtle doves or young pigeons.

[Leviticus 15:14, 29; Numbers 6:10; Luke 2:24]

15 The priest shall present them on the offering stand, and then wring off their heads, drain them of all their blood on the side of the offering stand, and roast them on the offering stand.

[Leviticus 5:8-9; 17:13]

16 He shall remove the crop and the feathers and dump them on the east side of the offering stand, the place for oily ashes.

17 The priest shall tear them open by their wings, but not tear them apart. Then he shall roast them over the burning firewood on the offering stand for burnt offerings as a sweet-savory roasted offering to Jehovah.

[Leviticus 1:8, 12]

CHAPTER 2

1 When anyone presents a grain offering to Jehovah, it shall be fine flour sprinkled with oil and frankincense.

[Leviticus 2:15]

2 He shall bring it to Aaron and his sons, the priests, and the *(officiating)* priest shall roast a token of it, that is, a handful of the fine flour sprinkled with oil and frankincense, on the offering stand as a sweet-savory roasted offering to Jehovah.

[Leviticus 2:9; 5:12; 6:15; Ephesians 5:2b; Philippians 4:18b]

3 The remainder of the grain offering, which is the holiest part of the roasted offering to Jehovah, shall belong to Aaron and his sons.

[Leviticus 2:10; 5:13b; 6:16a; 7:9; 24:8-9]

4 If your grain offering is baked in an oven, it should be of fine flour, either round unleavened cakes smeared with oil or unleavened wafers brushed with oil.

[Exodus 29:2, 23; Leviticus 8:26a]

5 If your grain offering is baked on a griddle, it should be of fine flour sprinkled with oil, but without yeast.

[Leviticus 2:11; 6:17a]

6 Break your grain offering into bite-size pieces and sprinkle oil on them.

[Leviticus 6:21a]

7 If your grain offering is cooked in a pan, it should be of fine flour sprinkled with oil.

8 Bring to Jehovah the grain offering prepared in any of these ways, and hand it to the priest who shall present it on the offering stand.

9 The priest shall roast a token of it, that is, a handful of the grain offering, on the offering stand as a sweet-savory roasted offering to Jehovah.

[Leviticus 2:2; 6:15; Ephesians 5:2b; Philippians 4:18b]

10 The remainder of the grain offering, which is the holiest part of the roasted offering to Jehovah, shall belong to Aaron and his sons.

[Leviticus 2:3; 5:13b; 6:16a; 7:10; 24:8-9]

11 Never present a grain offering made with yeast to Jehovah; never add yeast or honey to any of your roasted offerings to Jehovah.

[Leviticus 2:4-5, 11; 6:17a]

12 You may offer them as an offering of first fruits to Jehovah, but not to be roasted on the offering stand for a sweet savor.

[Leviticus 2:14]

13 Season with salt every grain offering of yours. Do not let the salt of God's covenant be lacking in it. Add salt to all your offerings.

[Numbers 18:19; Ezekiel 43:24]

14 Now if you offer a grain offering of first fruits to Jehovah, it should be fresh grain, grits of new growth.

[Leviticus 2:12, 16]

15 You must sprinkle oil and frankincense on such grain offering of yours.

[Leviticus 2:1]

16 And the priest shall roast a token of it, that is, a handful of the grits sprinkled with oil and frankincense, as a roasted offering to Jehovah.

CHAPTER 3

1 If his fellowship sacrifice to Jehovah is from the herd, it should either be a male *(bull)* or a female *(cow)* without defect.

[Exodus 29:10; Leviticus 1:3b; 8:14]

2 He shall lay his hand on the head of his offering, and it shall be slaughtered at the entrance of the tabernacle. Then Aaron's sons the priests shall spatter the blood all over the offering stand.

[Exodus 29:10-11; Leviticus 1:4a, 5; 4:4, 15; 8:14-15a; 9:18; 17:3-6a]

3 He shall roast all the fat of the fellowship sacrifice as a roasted offering to Jehovah, such as the fat blanketing the intestines, **4** the fat removed from the 2 kidneys and from the lobes of liver, as well as that from the hips.

[Exodus 29:13a; Leviticus 4:8-9; 7:3-4; 8:16; 9:10, 19]

5 Then the sons of Aaron shall roast all of it over the burning firewood on the offering stand for burnt offerings as a sweet-savory roasted offering to Jehovah.

[Leviticus 1:8; 17:6b]

6 If his fellowship sacrifice to Jehovah is from the flock, it should either be a male *(ram)* or a female *(ewe)* without defect.

[Leviticus 22:19-21; Deuteronomy 15:21; 17:1; Malachi 1:13]

7 If he offers a male lamb as a sacrifice, he should personally present it before Jehovah.

8 He shall lay his hand on the head of his offering, and it shall be slaughtered at the entrance of the tabernacle. Then the sons of Aaron shall spatter its blood all over the offering stand.

[Leviticus 1:11; 3:7-8; 4:33; 7:2; 17:3-6a]

9 He shall present all the fat of the fellowship sacrifice as a roasted offering to Jehovah, such as the entire fat tail removed from the backbone, the fat blanketing the intestines, **10** the fat removed from the 2 kidneys and from the lobes of liver, as well as that from the hips.

[Leviticus 7:3-4; 9:19]

11 Then the priest shall roast all of it on the offering stand as a roasted offering to Jehovah.

[Leviticus 7:5; 9:20]

12 If he offers a kid goat, he should personally present it before God.

13 He shall lay his hand on its head, and it shall be slaughtered at the entrance of the tabernacle. And the sons of Aaron shall spatter its blood all over the offering stand.

[Leviticus 1:11; 3:8; 4:24; 7:2; 17:3-6a]

14 He shall present all the fat as a roasted offering to Jehovah, such as the fat blanketing the intestines, **15** the fat removed from the 2 kidneys and from the lobes of liver, as well as that from the hips.

[Leviticus 7:3-4]

16 And the priest shall roast all of it on the offering stand as a sweet-savory roasted offering. All the fat belongs to Jehovah.

[Genesis 4:4]

17 This shall be a lasting ordinance throughout your generations wherever you are: Never eat any fat or any blood."

[Genesis 9:4; Leviticus 7:24-27; 17:10-14; 19:26a; Deuteronomy 12:16, 23-25; 15:23; Acts 15:20, 29; 21:25]

CHAPTER 4

1 Jehovah went on to say to Moses:

2 "Say to the Israelites, 'This is when a person unintentionally violates any of the prohibited acts of Jehovah ---

3 If the anointed priest sins and brings guilt on the people, then he shall present a bull calf without defect as a sin offering to Jehovah, for the violation he has committed.

[Leviticus 1:3a; 4:14]

4 He shall bring the bull calf to the entrance of the tabernacle, lay his hand on its head, and slaughter it before Jehovah.

[Exodus 29:10-11; Leviticus 1:3b-4a, 5a; 3:1-2; 4:14-15; 8:14; 17:3-5]

5 Then the anointed priest shall take some of the calf's blood and bring it to the Holy Place.

[Leviticus 4:16]

6 And the priest shall spatter with his fingers the blood 7 times before Jehovah toward the curtain of the Most Holy Place.

[Leviticus 14:17]

7 Then the priest shall rub some of the calf's blood on the horns of the offering stand for scented incense before Jehovah, which is in the Most Holy Place *(not tent of meeting)*, and pour its remaining blood on the base of the offering stand for burnt offerings, which is at the entrance of the tabernacle.

[Exodus 27:1; 30:1; Leviticus 4:18; 9:9]

8 He shall remove all the fat from the bull calf as a sin offering, such as the fat blanketing the intestines, **9** the fat on the 2 kidneys and on the lobes of liver, as well as that on the hips.

[Leviticus 3:3-4; 7:3-4; 8:16a; 9:10, 19]

10 It shall be the same as what was removed from the bull calf as a fellowship sacrifice. Then the priest shall roast all of it on the offering stand for burnt offerings.

[Leviticus 3:5; 4:19; 7:5; 8:16b; 9:10, 20]

11 But the calf's skin, all its flesh, along with its head, legs, entrails, and intestines, **12** that is, the bull calf as whole, shall be taken out of the camp and be brought to a clean place, where the oily ashes are dumped, and there all of it be burned over a burning firewood. Where the oily ashes are dumped, there it shall be burned.

[Exodus 29:14; Leviticus 4:21; 8:17; 9:11; 16:27; Hebrews 13:11]

13 This is when the whole Israelite community unintentionally violates any of the prohibited acts of Jehovah and thereby become guilty, although the community is not aware of it ---

14 On realizing the violation they have committed, the community shall present a bull calf as a sin offering and bring it to the entrance of the tabernacle.

[Exodus 29:10a; Leviticus 4:3-4a; 17:3-4]

15 And the elders of the community shall lay their hands on the calf's head, and it shall be slaughtered before Jehovah.

[Exodus 29:10b; Leviticus 1:4a, 5a; 3:2; 4:4b; 8:14-15a]

16 Then the anointed priest shall bring some of the calf's blood to the Holy Place.

[Leviticus 4:5]

17 The priest shall spatter with his fingers the blood 7 times before Jehovah toward the curtain.

[Leviticus 4:6]

18 Then he shall rub the blood on the horns of the offering stand *(for scented incense-see Verse 7a)* before Jehovah, which is in Most Holy Place, and pour the remaining blood on the base of the offering stand for burnt offerings, which is at the entrance of the tabernacle.

[Exodus 27:1; 29:12; 30:1; Leviticus 4:7; 9:9]

19 Then he shall remove all the fat from it and roast all of it on the offering stand.

[Exodus 29:13; Leviticus 3:5; 4:8-10; 7:3-5; 8:16; 9:10, 20]

20 The priest shall do to this calf what he did to the other calf as a sin offering. In this way the priest has taken away their sin, and they shall be pardoned.

[Leviticus 9:7; 16:27; Hebrews 9:12-14]

21 Then he shall have the bull calf *(as whole-see Verses 11 & 12)* be taken out of the camp and there be burned, just like the first calf as a sin offering for the community.

[Exodus 29:14; Leviticus 4:12; 8:17; 9:11; 16:27; Hebrews 13:11-12]

22 This is when a chieftain unintentionally violates any of the prohibited acts of Jehovah his God and thereby become guilty --
-

23 On realizing the violation he has committed, he shall bring a male kid goat without defect as his offering.

[Leviticus 4:23; 22:19-21; Deuteronomy 15:21; 17:1; Malachi 1:13]

24 He shall lay his hand on the head of the kid goat as a sin offering, and slaughter it at the place where burnt offerings are slaughtered before Jehovah.

[Leviticus 1:11a; 3:13]

25 Then the priest shall rub with his fingers the blood of the sin offering on the horns of the offering stand for burnt offerings, and pour the remaining blood on the base of the offering stand.

26 Just like the fat of the fellowship sacrifice, the priest shall roast all its fat on the offering stand. In this way the priest has taken away his sin, and he shall be pardoned.

27 This is when a citizen of the land unintentionally violates any of the prohibited acts of God and thereby become guilty ---

[Leviticus 4:35b]

28 On realizing that he has committed a violation, he shall bring a female kid goat without defect as his offering, for the violation he has committed.
29 He shall lay his hand on the head of the sin offering, and slaughter it at the place where burnt offerings are slaughtered.

[Leviticus 1:11a; 3:13]

30 Then the priest shall rub the blood on the horns of the offering stand for burnt offerings, and pour the remaining blood on the base of the offering stand.

31 The priest shall remove all its fat, just like what was removed from the fellowship sacrifice, and roast all of it on the offering stand for a sweet savor to Jehovah.

[Leviticus 3:14-16; 7:3-5; 17:6b]

In this way the priest has taken his sin, and he will be pardoned.

[Leviticus 17:11; Matthew 26:28; Hebrews 9:12-22]

32 If he offers a lamb as a sin offering, it should be a female without defect.

33 And he shall lay his hand on the head of the sin offering and slaughter it at the place where burnt offerings are slaughtered.

[Leviticus 3:8]

34 Then the priest shall rub with his fingers some of the blood of the sin offering on the horns of the offering stand for burnt offerings, and pour the remaining blood on the base of the offering stand.

35 The priest shall remove all its fat, just as the fat of the male sheep as a fellowship sacrifice was removed, and roast all of it on the offering stand as a roasted offering to Jehovah.

[Leviticus 3:11; 7:3-5]

In this way the priest has taken away his sin, that is, the violation he has committed, and he shall be pardoned.

[Leviticus 4:27]

CHAPTER 5

1 Now when a person who has heard a curse, firsthand or secondhand, refuses to report it, he shall be held liable.

[Leviticus 24:14; 1 Samuel 3:13; Proverbs 29:24]

2 A person who touches something unclean, whether the dead body of an unclean wild animal or an unclean farm animal, or the carcass of an unclean swarming insect, although he is not aware of it, he shall be unclean and thereby become guilty.

[Leviticus 11:31, 39]

3 One who touches any human uncleanness, whatever uncleanness it may be that made him unclean, although he is not aware of it, he becomes guilty once he realizes it.

4 A person who makes a promise recklessly, whether to do evil or to do good, whatever it may be that he swears recklessly of, although he is not aware of it, he becomes guilty once he realizes it.

5 If anyone is guilty of any of these things, he shall confess which sin in particular has he committed.

[Numbers 5:7a; Psalms 32:5; Proverbs 28:13; 1 John 1:9]

6 Then he shall bring a female from the flock, either a female lamb or a female kid goat, as a guilt offering to Jehovah for his sin, that is, the violation he has committed. And by it the priest shall take away his sin.

[Leviticus 4:31b, 35b; 5:6]

7 But if he cannot afford a lamb, then he shall bring 2 turtle doves or 2 young pigeons as a guilt offering to Jehovah for the violation he has committed; the one as a sin offering and the other as a burnt offering.

[Leviticus 12:8a; 14:30-31a]

8 He shall bring them to the priest, who shall first present the one as a sin offering. He shall wring off its head at the front of its neck, but not chop it off.

[Leviticus 1:14-15a]

9 Then he shall spatter some of the blood of the sin offering all over the offering stand and pour the remaining blood on the base of the offering stand.

[Leviticus 17:6a]

10 And in accordance with the usual procedure, the priest shall present the other one as a burnt offering. And by it he has taken away his sin, that is, the violation he has committed, and he shall be pardoned.

11 But if he cannot afford 2 turtle doves or 2 young pigeons, then he shall bring 1/10 of an ephah of fine flour as a sin offering for the violation he has committed. He must not sprinkle oil and frankincense on it because it is a sin offering.

12 He shall bring the sin offering to the priest, and the priest shall roast a token of it on the offering stand as a roasted offering to Jehovah.

13 And by it the priest has taken away his sin, that is, the violation he has committed, any of the prohibited acts, and he shall be pardoned. The remainder shall belong to the priest, just like the grain offering."

[Leviticus 2:3, 10; 6:17b; 10:12; 24:8-9]

14 Jehovah went on to say to Moses:

15 "When a person unintentionally mishandles the holy things of Jehovah, he shall bring a guilt offering to Jehovah, a male sheep without defect, to be assessed in silver shekels according to the standard sanctuary shekel.

[Leviticus 5:18; 6:6; 22:19-21; Deuteronomy 15:21; 17:1; Malachi 1:13; 1 Peter 1:18-19]

16 And he shall make compensation in full for mishandling the holy things and add 1/5 to the value, which he shall give to the priest.

[Leviticus 6:5b; 22:14; 27:13, 19; Numbers 5:7]

And by the male sheep as a guilt offering the priest has taken away his sin, and he shall be pardoned.

[Leviticus 6:6-7; 19:21-22]

17 A person who violates any of the prohibited acts of Jehovah, although he is not aware of it, is guilty and shall be held liable.

[Leviticus 5:1-4]

18 Although his sin is unintentional, he shall bring a male sheep without defect as a guilt offering to be assessed by the priest. And by it the priest has taken away his sin, his unintentional sin, for he was not aware of it, and he shall be pardoned.

[Leviticus 5:18; 6:6; 22:19-21]

19 It is a guilt offering because he is guilty before Jehovah.

CHAPTER 6

1 Jehovah went on to say to Moses:

2 "A person becomes unfaithful to Jehovah if he deceives his fellowman about anything he has entrusted to him, either he stole it or he took it by fraud;

3 or if he finds a lost thing and denies it, even lying under oath, or anything that makes him sin.

4 If he is found guilty, he must return the thing that was entrusted to him, which he stole or took by fraud, or the lost thing that he found *but denies it (see Verse 3)*;

5 or anything about which he lied about under oath.

And he shall make compensation in full, plus 1/5 to its value, and give it to the owner on the day he was found guilty.

[Leviticus 5:16a; 22:14; 27:13, 19; Numbers 5:7]

6 Then he must bring to Jehovah a guilt offering from the flock, a male sheep without defect, to be assessed by the priest.

[Leviticus 5:15, 18; 22:19-21; Deuteronomy 15:21; 17:1; Malachi 1:13; 1 Peter 1:18-19]

7 And by it the priest has taken away his sin, that is, the crime he is guilty of, and he shall be pardoned.

[Leviticus 19:22]

8 Jehovah went on to say to Moses:

9 "Say to Aaron and his sons, 'These are the regulations for burnt offerings:

The burnt offering shall remain on the grill of the offering stand all night till morning, and the fire shall be kept burning.

[Leviticus 6:12-13]

10 The priest shall put on the linen shorts and the official linen robe.

[Leviticus 16:4a]

Then he shall take the ashes of the burnt offering that was devoured by fire and place all of it at the side of the offering stand.

11 Afterwards he shall change his clothes and bring the ashes to a clean place outside the camp.

[Leviticus 1:16; 4:12b]

12 The fire on the offering stand shall be kept burning; it must not be put out. Every morning the priest shall burn wood on it, match the parts of the burnt offering to one another, and roast all of it along with all the fat of the fellowship sacrifice.

[Exodus 29:17; Leviticus 1:8, 12; 6:9]

13 The fire on the offering stand shall be kept burning, it must not be put out.

[Leviticus 6:9]

14 These are the regulations for grain offerings:

The sons of Aaron shall present it before Jehovah on the offering stand.

15 One of them shall roast a token, that is, a handful of the fine flour sprinkled with oil and frankincense, on the offering stand as a sweet-savory grain offering to Jehovah.

[Leviticus 2:2, 9; 6:15; 9:17; Ephesians 5:2b; Philippians 4:18b]

16 The remainder of it shall be made into unleavened cakes, which Aaron and his sons must eat in a holy place; they shall eat it at the courtyard of the tabernacle.

[Leviticus 6:26; 10:12-13a; 24:8-9]

17 It should not be baked with any yeast. I have given it as their share of the roasted offerings to Me. Like the sin offering and the guilt offering, it *(the remainder)* is the holiest part.

[Leviticus 2:4-5, 11; 6:17; 10:13b]

18 Every male descendant of Aaron shall eat of it. It is their share of the roasted offerings to Jehovah throughout their generations. Whatever touches them shall become holy."

[Numbers 18:10]

19 Jehovah went on to say to Moses:

20 "On the day Aaron is anointed, he and his sons shall present to Jehovah 1/10 of an ephah of fine flour as a grain offering daily, one half in the morning and one half in the evening.

21 It shall be baked with oil on a griddle. Break it into bite-size pieces and present all of it as a sweet-savory grain offering to Jehovah.

[Leviticus 2:5-6, 9; 6:15; Ephesians 5:2b; Philippians 4:18b]

22 This is a lasting ordinance: The anointed priest, any of his sons who succeeded him, shall roast all of it as a whole offering to Jehovah.

23 Every grain offering of a priest shall be offered all; none of it may be eaten."

24 Jehovah went on to say to Moses:

25 "Say to Aaron and his sons, 'These are the regulations for sin offerings:

The sin offering shall be slaughtered before Jehovah at the place where burnt offerings are slaughtered. It is most holy.

[Leviticus 4:29, 33; 6:25, 29b]

26 The priest who presents it as a sin offering must eat it in a holy place; it shall be eaten at the courtyard of the tabernacle.

[Leviticus 7:7]

27 Whatever touches its meat shall become holy. If its blood gets on somebody's clothes, it should be washed in a holy place.

28 The clay pot in which it was boiled shall be shattered. If it was boiled in a bronze pot, it should be scrubbed and rinsed with water.

29 Every male among the priests must eat of it; it is most holy.

[Numbers 18:10]

30 But no sin offering, which blood was brought to the tabernacle by which to take away sin, may be eaten; it must be burned.

[Leviticus 4:5, 16; 9:7; Hebrews 13:11]

CHAPTER 7

1 These are the regulations for guilt offerings, which are most holy:

2 The guilt offering shall be slaughtered at the place where burnt offerings are slaughtered, and its blood shall be spattered all over the offering stand.

3 All its fat shall be offered, such as the fat tail, the fat blanketing the intestines, **4** the fat removed from the 2 kidneys and from the lobes of liver, as well as that from the hips.

5 And the priest shall roast the guilt offering on the offering stand as a roasted offering to Jehovah.

6 Every male among the priests must eat of it. It shall be eaten in a holy place, it is most holy.

7 This regulation applies to both the sin offering and the guilt offering: The priest who takes away sins by it shall have them.

[Leviticus 6:26]

8 The priest who presents a burnt offering for someone else shall have for himself the skin of the animal sacrifice that he is presenting.

9 Every grain offering that is baked in an oven or on a griddle or cooked in a pan shall belong to the priest who presents it.

[Leviticus 5:13b]

10 And every grain offering, whether sprinkled with oil or dry, shall be shared equally among the sons of Aaron.

[Leviticus 2:3, 10; 6:16a; 7:10; 24:9]

11 These are the regulations for fellowship sacrifices to Jehovah:

12 If one offers it as an expression of gratitude, he shall present it along with round cakes smeared with oil and unleavened wafers brushed with oil. Break it into bite size pieces and sprinkle oil on them.

[Exodus 29:2, 23; Leviticus 2:4-6]

13 More so, he shall present his fellowship sacrifice for thanksgiving along with loaves of unleavened bread.

14 He shall present each kind as a heave offering *(offering that was pulled out)* to Jehovah, and it shall belong to the priest who spattered the blood of the fellowship sacrifice.

15 And the meat of the fellowship sacrifice for thanksgiving must be eaten on the very day it is offered. None of it may be saved till morning.

[Exodus 12:8a, 10a; 23:18b; 34:25b; Leviticus 22:30; Numbers 9:12a; Deuteronomy 16:4b]

16 If his fellowship sacrifice is a vow or a freewill offering, it must be eaten on the very day he offered it.

What is left of it on the 2nd day may still be eaten, **17** but what is left of the meat of the fellowship sacrifice till the 3rd day must be burned.

[Exodus 12:10b; 29:34; Leviticus 8:32; 19:6b]

18 If ever any of the meat of the fellowship sacrifice is eaten on the 3rd day, he who offers it would not be accepted with approval. It will not be credited to him. It is spoiled, the person who eats of it shall be held liable.

[Leviticus 19:7-8]

19 And the meat that have come into contact with anything unclean must not be eaten; it is to be burned up. As for the clean meat, anyone may eat it.

20 The person who eats the meat of the fellowship sacrifice which is for Jehovah, while he is unclean, shall be purged from his people.

21 A person who touches whatever unclean, whether human uncleanness or an unclean animal or any other unclean detestable creature, and eats the meat of the fellowship sacrifice which is for Jehovah shall be purged from his people."

22 Jehovah went on to say to Moses:

23 "Say to the Israelites, 'You must not eat any fat, whether the fat of a bull calf or of a male lamb or of a kid goat.

[Genesis 4:4; Leviticus 3:16b-17]

24 The fat of an animal found dead or mangled may be put to any other use, but never must you eat it.

25 The person who eats the fat of the animal that he is presenting as a roasted offering to Jehovah shall be purged from his people.

26 You must not eat any blood, whether that of bird or that of an animal, wherever you are.

[Genesis 9:4; Leviticus 17:11-14; Deuteronomy 12:16, 23-25; 15:23; Acts 15:20, 29; 21:25]

27 The person who eats any blood shall be purged from his people."

[Leviticus 17:10]

28 Jehovah went on to say to Moses:

29 "Say to the Israelites, 'He who offers a fellowship sacrifice shall personally bring it to Jehovah.

30 He shall bring the fat on the breast as a roasted offering to Jehovah. He shall bring it with the breast and wave it as a wave offering before Jehovah.

[Exodus 29:26; Leviticus 8:29]

31 The priest shall roast the fat on the offering stand, but the breast shall belong to Aaron and his sons.

[Leviticus 9:20; 10:14]

32 Give to the priest the right leg that was pulled out from your fellowship sacrifice.

[Leviticus 10:14]

33 Anyone of the sons of Aaron who presents the blood and the fat of the fellowship sacrifice shall have the right leg as his share.

34 By a lasting ordinance, I take the breast that was waved and the leg that was pulled out from the fellowship sacrifices of the Israelites, and give them to Aaron the priest and his sons.

[Exodus 29:27]

35 These *(the breast and the leg)* are the share due the priests, Aaron and his sons, of the roasted offerings to Jehovah from the day they were presented to serve as priests to Jehovah.

36 Just as Jehovah had told, the Israelites shall give these to them on the day they were anointed. This is a lasting ordinance throughout your generations.'"

37 These, then, are the regulations for burnt offerings, for grain offerings, for sin offerings, for guilt offerings, for ordination offerings, and for fellowship sacrifices, **38** just as Jehovah had instructed Moses in Mount Sinai on the day the Israelites were told to offer *(animal)* sacrifices in the wilderness of Sinai.

CHAPTER 8

1 Jehovah went on to say to Moses:

2 "Bring Aaron and his sons, their garments, the anointing oil, the bull as a sin offering, the two male sheep, and the basket containing unleavened bread, **3** and gather the whole community at the entrance of the tabernacle."

4 And Moses did so, just as Jehovah had told him; the community was gathered at the entrance of the tabernacle.

5 Now Moses said to the community: "This is the step-by-step procedure given by Jehovah."

[Leviticus 8:34]

6 *First,* Moses presented Aaron and his sons and washed them with water.

[Exodus 29:4]

7 *Second,* he put the sleeveless robe on him, then the *checkered* coat, and tied the sash of the ephod to him.

[Exodus 29:5]

8 *Third,* he put the breastplate on him and set on it the Urim *(indicating 'Guilty')* and the Thummim *(indicating 'Innocent')*.

[Exodus 29:5]

9 *Fourth,* Moses set the turban on his head and tied the shiny golden plate, that is, the label of holiness, to the front of the turban, just as Jehovah had told him.

[Exodus 29:6]

10 *Fifth,* Moses anointed the tabernacle and all that is in it with the anointing oil, thus sanctifying them.

[Exodus 30:26-28]

11 *Sixth,* he spattered some of the oil on the offering stand 7 times, thus anointing and sanctifying the offering stand and all its utensils, as well as the washbasin with stand.

[Exodus 30:28]

12 Lastly, he poured some of the oil on the head of Aaron, thus anointing and sanctifying him.

[Exodus 29:7]

13 Next Moses presented the sons of Aaron and put the robes on them, tied the sashes to them, and wrapped the turbans around their heads, just as Jehovah had told him.

[Exodus 29:8-9]

14 Afterwards he presented the bull calf as a sin offering, and Aaron and his sons laid their hands on its head.

[Exodus 29:10]

15 Moses slaughtered it and rubbed with his fingers the blood on all the horns of the offering stand, and thus cleansed it from sin. Then he poured the remaining blood on the base of the offering stand and thus sanctified it from sin.

[Exodus 29:11-12]

16 Afterwards Moses removed all the fat, such as the flat blanketing the intestines and the fat on the lobes of liver and on the 2 kidneys, and roasted all of it on the offering stand.

[Exodus 29:13]

17 Moses have the calf's skin, its flesh, and its intestines be burned outside the camp, just as Jehovah had told him.

[Exodus 29:14]

18 Then he presented the male sheep as a burnt offering, and Aaron and his sons laid their hands on its head.

[Exodus 29:15]

19 Afterwards Moses slaughtered it and spattered its blood all over the offering stand.

[Exodus 29:16]

20 Then Moses cut the sheep into parts, matched the parts to one another up its head *(see Exodus 29:17a,)* and roasted all this along with all the fat.

21 Moses washed the entrails and legs with water and roasted the lamb as whole on the offering stand for burnt offerings, as a sweet-savory roasted offering to Jehovah, just as Jehovah had told him.

[Exodus 29:17b-18]

22 Then he presented the other male sheep, the sheep of ordination, and Aaron and his sons laid their hands on its head.

[Exodus 29:19]

23 Afterwards Moses slaughtered it and rubbed some of its blood on the lobe of Aaron's right ear, on the thumb of his right hand, and on the big toe of his right foot.

[Exodus 29:20a]

24 Next Moses presented the sons of Aaron and rubbed some of the blood on the lobes of their right ears, on the thumbs of their right hands, and on the big toes of their right feet. But the remaining blood he spattered all over the offering stand.

[Exodus 29:20b]

25 Then he took all the fat, such as the fat tail, the fat blanketing the intestines, the fat on the lobes of the liver and on the 2 kidneys, as well as the right leg.

[Exodus 29:22]

26 He also took a loaf of unleavened bread, a round cake smeared with oil, and a wafer from the basket that was before

Jehovah, and placed all of it on top of the fat parts and the right leg.

[Exodus 29:23]

27 After that he handed them all to Aaron and his sons and waved them as a wave offering before Jehovah.

[Exodus 29:24]

28 Then Moses took them from their hands and roasted them on the offering stand for burnt offerings as a sweet-savory ordination offering to Jehovah.

[Exodus 29:25]

29 And Moses took the breast of the sheep of ordination and waved it as a wave offering before Jehovah, which shall be his share, just as Jehovah had told him.

[Exodus 29:26]

30 Afterwards Moses took some of the anointing oil and some of the blood from the offering stand and spattered these on Aaron and his garments, and on his sons and their garments, thus sanctifying Aaron and his garments, and his sons and their garments.

[Exodus 29:21]

31 Then Moses told Aaron and his sons: "Roast the meat at the entrance of the tabernacle and there you shall eat it, along with

the bread from the basket of ordination, just as I was told, saying, 'Aaron and his sons shall eat it.'

[Exodus 29:31-32]

32 And what is left of the meat and of the bread burn up.

[Exodus 29:34a]

33 You must not leave the tabernacle until you have completed the days of your ordination, which will take 7 days.

[Exodus 29:35]

34 This, then, is the step-by-step procedure given by Jehovah so that your sins shall be taken away.

[Leviticus 8:5]

35 Stay at the tabernacle day and night for 7 days. Perform your obligatory duty to Jehovah that you may not die, for so I have been told."

[Leviticus 10:7]

36 Thus Moses did everything to Aaron and his sons just as Jehovah had told him.

[Leviticus 29:35]

CHAPTER 9

1 On the 8th day, Moses called Aaron, his sons, and the elders of Israel.

2 He told Aaron: "Present to Jehovah a bull calf as a sin offering and a male sheep as a burnt offering, both without defect.

[Leviticus 1:2; 22:19-21; Deuteronomy 15:21; 17:1; Malachi 1:13]

3 Then tell the Israelites, 'Bring a male kid goat as a sin offering, a bull calf and a male lamb, both a year old without defect, as a burnt offering;

4 another bull calf and a male lamb as a fellowship sacrifice to Jehovah, along with a grain offering sprinkled with oil, because today Jehovah will meet with you."

5 Thus they brought to the entrance of the tabernacle all what Moses has mentioned. Then the whole community came and presented themselves before Jehovah.

[Leviticus 17:3-4]

6 Moses said: "These are what Jehovah has commanded you to do so you will see the glory of Jehovah."

7 Then Moses told Aaron: "Go to the offering stand and present your sin offering and your burnt offering by which to take away your sins and those of your household. Then present the offering of the people by which to take away their sins, just as Jehovah has told."

[Leviticus 1:4; 4:20, 26b, 31c, 35c; 6:6-7; 16:6, 11; 19:22]

8 Right away Aaron went to the offering stand and slaughtered the calf as his sin offering.

[Leviticus 1:5a; 4:15; 7:2a; 9:12a, 18a]

9 Then the sons of Aaron handed the blood to him, and he rubbed the blood with his fingers on the horns of the offering stand, and poured the remaining blood on the base of the offering stand.

[Exodus 29:12; Leviticus 4:18; 8:15]

10 And Moses roasted on the offering stand the fat that was removed from the kidneys and from the liver as a sin offering, just as Jehovah had told him.

[Exodus 29:13; Leviticus 3:3-5; 4:8-10, 19; 7:3-5; 8:16; 9:19-20]

11 He burned the flesh and the skin outside the camp.

[Exodus 29:14; Leviticus 4:11-12, 21; 8:17; 16:27; Hebrews 13:11]

12 Then he slaughtered the burnt offering, and the sons of Aaron handed him the blood, and he spattered it all over the offering stand.

[Exodus 29:16; Leviticus 1:5; 3:2; 4:15; 7:2; 9:18; 17:6a]

13 And they handed him the body parts and the head of the burnt offering, and he roasted all of it on the offering stand.

[Exodus 29:17a; Leviticus 1:6b-7]

14 More so, he washed the entrails and legs and roasted them altogether on the offering stand for burnt offerings.

[Exodus 29:17b-18; Leviticus 1:9]

15 Next he presented the goat as the people's sin offering and slaughtered it just like the first one.

[Leviticus 1:10-11a]

16 Then he presented the burnt offering in accordance with the usual procedure.

17 Next he presented the grain offering and roasted a token of it on the offering stand, aside from the burnt offering in the morning.

[Leviticus 2:2, 9; 6:15]

18 Afterwards Aaron slaughtered the bull and the male sheep as the people's fellowship sacrifice. Then the sons of Aaron handed him the blood, and he spattered it all over the offering stand.

[Leviticus 1:5, 11; 3:2, 8; 4:15, 33; 7:2; 8:19; 9:12, 18; 17:6a]

19 All the fat of the bull and of the male sheep, such as the fat tail, the fat blanketing the intestines, and the fat on the 2 kidneys and on the lobes of liver **20** including the fat on the breast, he roasted on the offering stand.

[Exodus 29:13, 22; Leviticus 3:3-5, 9-11; 4:8-10, 19; 7:3-5; 8:16, 25, 28; 9:10, 19-20]

21 But the breast and the right leg Aaron waved as a wave offering before Jehovah, just as Jehovah had told.

[Exodus 29:27; Leviticus 9:21]

22 After laying his hands on the people and blessing them, Aaron stepped down from presenting the sin offerings, the burnt offerings, and the fellowship sacrifice.

23 Finally Moses and Aaron entered the tabernacle, and then came out and blessed the people. Then the glory of Jehovah was seen by all the people.

24 And fire came out from before Jehovah and devoured the burnt offerings and the fat parts on the offering stand. When the people saw it, a chorus of shouts broke out, and they fell facedown.

[1 Kings 18:38-39; 2 1 Chronicles 21:26; 2 Chronicles 7:1-3]

CHAPTER 10

1 Not long thereafter Aaron's sons, Nadab and Abihu, brought their own incense burners and burned incense in them. However, they burned incense to Jehovah without Him authorizing them.

2 Thus a fire came out from before Jehovah, and they died before Him.

[Leviticus 10:6; 16:13; Numbers 26:61; 1 Chronicles 24:2a]

3 So Moses said to Aaron: This is what Jehovah says, 'Those who come to Me should give Me glory before the eyes of all the people."

[Leviticus 22:32]

And Aaron just kept silent.

4 Then Moses called Mishael and Elzaphan, the sons of Uzziel (Aaron's uncle), and told them: "Come here, take your nephews from the Most Holy Place and bring them out of the camp."

[Exodus 6:22]

5 Thus they carried them in their robes and brought them outside the camp, just as Moses has told.

6 After that Moses told Aaron and his remaining sons, Eleazar and Ithamar: "Do not leave your hair uncombed and do not rend your garments, that you may die, and that He may not get angry against the whole community. Let your kinsmen of the house of Israel do the weeping over the burning that Jehovah has brought about.

[Leviticus 10:2; 21:10]

7 And do not leave the tabernacle, or you shall die, because the anointing oil of Jehovah is poured on you."

[Leviticus 8:35]

   And they did what Moses said.
8 Then Jehovah told Aaron:

9 "When you go to the tabernacle, do not drink wine or liquor, you and your sons, or you shall die. This is a lasting ordinance throughout your generations.

[Isaiah 28:7; Ezekiel 44:21]

10 This is so that you may distinguish holy from profane, and clean from unclean, 11 and so you can teach the Israelites all the regulations that Jehovah has laid on them through Moses."

[Leviticus 11:47; 14:57]

12 Then Moses told Aaron and his remaining sons, Eleazar and Ithamar: "Take the remainder of the grain offering, which is the holiest part of the roasted offering to Jehovah, and eat it unleavened near the offering stand.

[Leviticus 2:3-5, 10-11;, 6:17b]

13 You shall eat it in a holy place, for that is your share and your sons' share of the roasted offerings to Jehovah, just as I have been told.

[Leviticus 6:16-18a; 24:8-9; Numbers 18:10]

14 And you, your sons, and your daughters shall eat the breast that was waved and the leg that was pulled out in a holy place, for these have been given as your share and your children's share from the Israelites' fellowship sacrifices.

[Exodus 29:27-28; Leviticus 7:34]

15 The leg that was pulled out and the breast that was waved shall be brought, along with the fat parts that were roasted, and be waved as a wave offering before Jehovah. These shall be your perpetual share, you and your sons, just as Jehovah had told."

[Leviticus 7:35; 9:21]

16 But when Moses looked for the goat as a sin offering, it has been burned!

Enraged with Eleazar and Ithamar, Aaron's remaining sons, he said:

17 "Why did you not eat the sin offering in a holy place? He has given it to you because it is the holiest part, by which you can take away the sins of the community before Jehovah!

18 Since its blood has not been brought to a holy place, by all means you should have eaten it in a holy place, just as I have been told!"

[Leviticus 6:26, 29]

19 At that Aaron answered Moses: "Look, today, as they were presenting their sin offering and burnt offering before Jehovah, this thing befell me. Had I eaten the sin offering today, would it be alright to Jehovah?"

20 And Moses was satisfied with the answer.

CHAPTER 11

1 Now Jehovah told Moses and Aaron:

2 "Say to the Israelites, 'Of the land animals, you may eat **3** any animal that is cloven-footed and that chews the cud *(regurgitates partially digested food from the 1st stomach and back to the mouth for a 2nd chewing).*

[Deuteronomy 14:6]

4 But you may not eat those that chew the cud but are not cloven-footed, and those that are cloven-footed but do not chew the cud, such as follows:

the camel, it chews the cud but is not cloven-footed; regard it as unclean; **[Deuteronomy 14:7]**

5 the rock badger, it chews the cud but is not cloven-footed; regard it as unclean; **[Deuteronomy 14:7]**

6 the rabbit, it chews the cud but is not cloven-footed; regard it as unclean; **[Deuteronomy 14:7]**

7 and the pig, it is cloven-footed but does not chew the cud; regard it as unclean. **[Deuteronomy 14:8a]**

8 Do not eat any of their meat and you must not touch their dead body; regard them as unclean.

[Deuteronomy 14:8b]

9 Of the marine animals, whether in seas or in rivers, you may eat all that have fins and scales.

[Deuteronomy 14:9]

10 All marine animals that do not have fins and scales, such as shellfish and jellyfish, whether in seas or in rivers, you are to detest.

[Deuteronomy 14:10]

11 Yes, you are to detest them. You must not eat any of their flesh, and you are to detest their dead body.

[Deuteronomy 14:3]

12 Every marine animal that has no fins and scales regard as detestable.

[Deuteronomy 14:10]

13 Of the flying animals dislike and do not eat the following, for they are detestable:

> the eagle, the sea hawk, the black vulture
> **[Deuteronomy 14:12]**

14 the red kite, any kind of black kite **[Deuteronomy 14:13]**

15 any kind of raven **[Deuteronomy 14:14]**

16 the ostrich, the short-eared owl, the seagull, any kind of falcon **[Deuteronomy 14:15]**

17 the little owl, the cormorant, the long-eared owl **[Deuteronomy 14:16]**

18 the swan, the pelican, the vulture **[Deuteronomy 14:17]**

19 the stork, any kind of heron, the hoopoe, and the bat **[Deuteronomy 14:18]**

20 Any winged swarming insect that goes on all fours regard as detestable.

[Deuteronomy 14:19]

21 Of the winged swarming insects that go on all fours, you may eat those that have jointed legs with which they jump on the ground.

22 Of them, you may eat migratory locust of any kind, edible locust of any kind, cricket of any kind, and grasshopper of any kind.

[Matthew 3:4b; Mark 1:6b]

23 Any other winged swarming insects that have 4 legs regard as detestable.

24 For by them you would make yourselves unclean. Whoever touches their carcasses shall be unclean till evening.

25 And whoever picks up any of their carcasses shall wash his clothes, and he shall be unclean till evening.

26 All animals that are not cloven-footed and do not chew the cud regard as unclean. Whoever touches them shall be unclean.

27 Of the land animals, any 4-footed animals that walks on their paws regard as unclean. Whoever touches their dead body shall be unclean till evening.

28 And anyone who carries their dead body shall wash his clothes, and he shall be unclean till evening. Regard them as unclean.

29 Of the creeping animals that creeps on the ground regard as unclean the naked mole-rat and the jerboa.

[Leviticus 11:41]

Of the reptiles, **30** the gecko, the monitor lizard, the common lizard, the sand lizard, and the chameleon.

[Proverbs 30:28]

31 Regard as unclean all reptiles. Whoever touches their dead body shall be unclean till evening.

32 Any object on which any of their carcasses falls shall be unclean, whether it is wood or cloth or leather or burlap. But if you need to use it, then soak it in water overnight, and then it shall be clean.

33 Any clay pot on which anyone of them falls, everything that is in it shall be unclean; smash it.

34 Any soup which water have been taken from the clay pot shall be unclean, and any drink in it shall be unclean.

35 Anything on which any of their carcasses falls shall be unclean. Whether it is a stove or jar, smash it. They are unclean, regard them as unclean.

36 Only a spring or a pool of running water shall remain clean; but whoever touches their carcasses shall be unclean.

37 If any of their carcasses falls on any plant seed which is to be sown, it is clean;

38 but if the seed is wet when any of their carcasses falls on it, regard it as unclean.

39 If any animal which you may eat dies, anyone who touches its dead body shall be unclean till evening.

40 And anyone who eats or carries any of its dead body shall wash his clothes, and he shall be unclean till evening.

[Leviticus 22:8]

41 Any creeping animal that creeps on the ground regard as detestable; they may not be eaten.

[Leviticus 11:29]

42 Of the winged swarming insects, you may not eat those that crawl on their belly and those that go on all fours or on many feet; they are detestable.

43 Do not make yourselves detestable by any swarming insect, and thus make yourselves unclean by them.

44 Because I Jehovah your God, am clean, you must cleanse yourselves and keep yourselves clean. Thus you must you make yourselves unclean by any creeping animal that creeps on the ground.

[Exodus 22:31a; Leviticus 19:2; 20:7, 26; Numbers 15:40; 1 Peter 1:15-16]

45 Yes, because Jehovah, who took you out of Egypt to be God to you, is clean, you must keep yourselves clean.

[Genesis 17:7-8; Exodus 6:7b; 29:45; Leviticus 26:12a; Deuteronomy 29:13; 2 Samuel 7:24; Jeremiah 7:23a; 11:4; 24:7; 30:22; 31:1a, 33; 32:38; Ezekiel 11:20; 14:11; 34:30; 36:28; 37:23, 27; Zechariah 8:8; 2 Corinthians 6:16; Hebrews 8:10]

46 These, then, are the regulations for land animals, for flying animals, for marine animals, and for swarming insects, *and for creeping animals* that creep on the ground, **47** so that you can distinguish clean from unclean, and animals that may be eaten from those that may not be eaten."

[Leviticus 10:10; 20:25]

CHAPTER 12

1 Jehovah went on to say to Moses:

2 "Say to the Israelites, 'A pregnant woman who gives birth to a baby boy shall be unclean 7 days, as unclean as when she is on her period.

3 And on the 8th day, *the newborn baby boy* shall be circumcised.

[Genesis 17:12a; Luke 1:59; 2:21; Acts 7:8; Philippians 3:5a]

4 It will take 33 days for her to be cleansed from blood. She should not touch any holy thing and she should not go to a holy place until the days of her cleansing is completed.

5 Now if she gives birth to a baby girl, then she shall be unclean 14 days, as unclean as when she is on her period. And it will take 66 days for her to be cleansed from blood.

6 When her days of cleansing is completed, either for a baby boy or for a baby girl, she must bring a one-year-old lamb as a burnt offering, and a young pigeon or a turtle dove as a sin offering, to the priest at the entrance of the tabernacle.

7 And she shall present it before Jehovah by which to cleanse her, and she shall be cleansed from blood.

These, then, are the regulations for her who gives birth, either to a male or to a female.

8 But if she cannot afford a lamb, then she must bring 2 turtle doves or 2 young pigeons, the one as a burnt offering and the other as a sin offering, by which the priest shall cleanse her, and she shall be clean."

[Leviticus 5:6-7; 14:30-31a]

CHAPTER 13

1 Jehovah went on to say to Moses and Aaron:

2 "When a man has a skin rash or a scab or a blotchy skin which could develop to a serious skin disease, he must be brought to Aaron the priest or to one of his sons who is priest.

3 And the priest must examine the skin disease. When the hairs in the diseased area have turned white and the disease appears to be deeper than the skin, it is a serious skin disease. After the priest examine it, he should pronounce him unclean.

[Leviticus 13:20]

4 But if the blotch on the skin is white, it does not appear deeper than the skin, and the hairs *on it* have not turned white, then the priest must quarantine the man 7 days.

[Leviticus 13:21]

5 On the 7th day the priest must examine him. If the skin disease is checked and has not spread, the priest must quarantine him another 7 days.

6 On the 7th day the priest must reexamine him. If the skin disease has become dull and has not spread, the priest should pronounce him clean. It was but a rash. And he shall wash his clothes and be clean.

7 But if the rash has spread on the skin, after the priest has pronounced him clean, he should see the priest again.

8 The priest shall take a look. If the skin rash has spread, then the priest shall pronounce him unclean. It is a serious skin disease.

9 And if a man has a serious skin disease, he must be brought to the priest.

10 The priest must take a look.

If there is a white eruption in the skin, which has turned the hairs *on it* white, and there is an open sore in the eruption, **11** then it is dermatitis. The priest shall pronounce him unclean. He need not quarantine him, he is obviously unclean.

12 But if the rash spreads all over his body, covering his body from head to foot, so far as the priest can see, **13** then the priest must take a look. If his body is covered in a rash, but have turned white, he should declare the rash cured. He is clean.

14 But when an open sore appears in *the rash*, then he shall be unclean.

15 After the priest examines the open sore, he shall pronounce him unclean, for sores are symptom of infection.

16 But if the open sore heals and *the rashes* have turned white, he should go to the priest.

17 And the priest must examine him. If the rashes have turned white, the priest should declare it cured. He is clean.

18 When someone has a boil on the skin and it heals, **19** but then a white spot or red spot appears where the boil was, he should see the priest.

20 And the priest must take a look. If it appears to be deeper than the skin and the hairs *on it* have turned white, the priest should pronounce him unclean. A skin disease has broken out in the boil.

[Leviticus 13:3]

21 But after the priest examines it, and there is no white hair in it, and it does not appear deeper than the skin and is dull, the priest must quarantine him 7 days.

[Leviticus 13:4]

22 If it spreads in the skin, the priest should pronounce him unclean; it is a skin disease.

23 But if the spot stays and has not spread, it is but the crust of the boil. The priest should pronounce him clean.

24 When the skin is burned by fire and the burn blister becomes reddish white or white, **25** the priest must examine it. If the hairs on the blister have turned white and it appears to be deeper than the skin, a skin disease has broken out in the blister. The priest should pronounce him unclean.

26 But after the priest examine it, and there is no white hair on the blister, it does not appear deeper than the skin and is dull, the priest must quarantine him 7 days.

27 On the 7th day the priest must reexamine him. If it spreads on the skin, then the priest shall pronounce him unclean. The blister does become infected.

28 But if the blister stays and has not spread, and is dull, it is but a burn mark. The priest should pronounce him clean; it is but a burn scar.

29 When a disease develops on the scalp or on the chin of a man or a woman, **30** the priest must examine the disease. If it appears to be deeper than the skin and the hairs in it are yellow and few, the priest should pronounce him/her unclean. It is a disease causing hair loss, either on the head or on the chin.

31 After the priest examines the disease causing hair loss, and it does not appear deeper than the skin, yet there is no black hair in it, the priest must quarantine him 7 days.

32 On the 7th day the priest must examine the disease.

If the disease causing hair loss has not spread, and no hair in it has turned yellow, and the disease does not appear deeper than the skin, **33** then he must shave his head, but without shaving the hair on the diseased area. And the priest must quarantine him another 7 days.

34 On the 7th day the priest shall reexamine the disease causing hair loss. If it has not spread and it does not appear deeper than the skin, the priest should pronounce him clean. He shall wash his clothes and be clean.

35 But if the disease causing hair loss spreads after he has been pronounced clean, **36** the priest must then examine him. If the disease has spread, the priest need not look for yellow hair, he is obviously unclean.

37 But if the disease causing hair loss stops and black hair has grown in it, then the disease has been cured. He is healed, and the priest should pronounce him clean.

38 When a person, male or female, has white spots on the skin, **39** the priest must take a look. If the spots on the skin are dull white, it is but a skin rash. He is clean.

40 When a man loses his hair and goes bald, he is clean.

41 When he loses his beard hair or cannot grow a beard, he is clean.

42 But if there are reddish-white spots on his bald scalp or bald chin, an infectious disease is breaking out on it.

43 And the priest must examine him.

If there are reddish-white spots on his bald scalp or bald chin, **44** he has infectious skin disease; he is unclean. The priest should pronounce him unclean, it is scalp psoriasis.

[Leviticus 14:2]

45 And the one who has such skin disease shall rend his garment, leave his hair uncombed, and shout out with covered mouth, saying, 'I am unclean, I am unclean!'

46 As long as he has the disease, he remains unclean. And as such, he should stay isolated; he should live outside the camp.

[Leviticus 14:3]

47 Now when bacteria lives in a garment, whether it is wool or linen, **48** either in the warp fibers *(vertical threads)* or in the weft fibers *(horizontal threads)* of the linen or of the wool, or in a leather or in anything made of leather, **49** and there is a yellowish-green or reddish stain in warp or in the weft of the garment or in any kind of leather, it is infected; it must be shown to the priest.

50 After the priest examines the infected item, he must isolate it 7 days.

51 On the 7th day he shall reexamine the infected item. If the stain has spread in the warp fibers or in the weft fibers, or in whatever leather it may be, it is persistent bacterial infection. It is unclean.

52 He must burn the warp fibers or the weft fibers of the garment, wool or linen, or anything made of leather in which the bacteria may thrive; it is persistent bacterial infection. It must be burned with fire.

[Leviticus 13:57]

53 But if the priest takes a look, and the stain has not spread in the warp fibers or in the weft fibers of the garment, or in anything made of leather, **54** the priest must have the infected item be washed. Then he must isolate it for another 7 days.

55 After the infected item has been washed, the priest shall reexamine the stain. If the stain is still there and went deeper into the fiber, although it has not spread, it is unclean. You should burn it with fire; it is infected inside out.

56 But after the priest takes a look, and the stain has faded after it has been washed, he should cut out the warp fibers or the weft fibers from the garment or from the leather.

57 But if it reappears in the warp fibers or in the weft fibers of the garment, or in anything made of leather, then it is growing *in numbers*. You should burn with fire whatever it is in which the stain is.

[Leviticus 13:52]

58 When the stain disappeared from the warp fibers or from the weft fibers of the garment, or from anything made of leather, after it had been washed, it must be washed again and it shall be clean.

59 These, then, are the regulations in pronouncing clean or unclean an infected garment, whether in the warp fibers or in the weft fibers of a garment, wool or linen, or in anything made of leather."

CHAPTER 14

1 Jehovah went on to say to Moses:

2 "This shall be the procedure when a person is cured of infectious skin disease and brought to the priest to be pronounced clean:

[Leviticus 14:43]

3 The priest shall go outside the camp to determine the condition of the person who is cured of infectious skin disease.

[Leviticus 13:46]

4 And the priest shall tell him to bring for his cleansing 2 live clean birds, cedar wood, red yarn, and hyssop.

[Leviticus 14:49]

5 Then the priest shall have one of the birds be drowned in a clay pot by running water.

[Leviticus 14:50]

6 As for the live bird, he shall dip it along with the cedar wood, the red yarn, and the hyssop in the blood of the bird that was drowned by running water.

[Leviticus 14:51-52]

7 He shall spatter the blood 7 times on the one who is cured of infectious skin disease and then pronounce him clean. Then he shall release the live bird into the open field.

[Leviticus 14:53a]

8 And the one seeking cleansing shall wash his clothes, shave off all his hair, and take a bath, and he shall be clean. After that he may enter the camp, but must stay first outside his tent 7 days.

9 On the 7th day he shall shave his head, his beard, and his eyebrows. Yes, he shall shave off all his hair, then wash his clothes and take a bath, and he shall be clean.

10 And on the 8th day he shall bring 2 male lambs and 1 female lamb, both one year old without defect, and 3/10 of an ephah of fine flour sprinkled with oil as a grain offering, and a log of oil.

[Leviticus 14:15]

11 The priest who pronounced him clean shall present the man seeking cleansing, as well as his offerings, before Jehovah at the entrance of the tabernacle.

12 Then the priest shall present one of the male lambs as a guilt offering, along with the log of oil, and wave them as a wave offering before Jehovah.

[Leviticus 14:24]

13 He shall slaughter the male lamb at the place where sin offerings and burnt offerings are slaughtered. And like the sin offering, the guilt offering shall belong to the priest; it is most holy.

14 The priest shall rub some of the blood of the guilt offering on the lobe of the right ear of the one seeking cleansing, on the thumb of his right hand, and on the big toe of his right foot.

[Leviticus 14:25]

15 Then the priest shall take the log of oil and pour some oil on his left palm.

[Leviticus 14:10]

16 The priest shall dip his right hand in the oil that is on his left palm, and spatter the oil with his fingers 7 times before Jehovah.

[Leviticus 14:26-27]

17 And the priest shall rub with his fingers the remaining oil on the lobe of the right ear of the one seeking cleansing, on the thumb of his right hand, and on the big toe of his right foot, over the blood of the guilt offering.

[Leviticus 14:28]

18 And the priest shall rub the remaining oil in his palm on the head of the one seeking cleansing. Then the priest shall take away his sin before Jehovah.

[Leviticus 14:29]

19 The priest shall present the sin offering by which to take away the sin of the one seeking cleansing, and then slaughter the burnt offering.

20 And together with the burnt offering, the priest shall present the grain offering on the offering stand. In this way the priest has taken away his sin, and he shall be clean.

21 Now if he is poor and does not have the means, then he must bring only one male lamb *(to be given back)* as a guilt offering by which to take away his sin, and 1/10 of an ephah of fine flour sprinkled with oil as a grain offering, a log of oil, **22** and two turtle doves or two young pigeons, whichever he can afford, the one as a sin offering and the other as a burnt offering.

23 On the 8th day, he shall bring them for his cleansing to the priest at the entrance of the tabernacle before Jehovah.

[Leviticus 17:3-4]

24 The priest shall take the male lamb as a guilt offering, and the log of oil, and wave them as a wave offering before Jehovah.

[Leviticus 14:12]

25 Then the priest shall slaughter the male lamb as a guilt offering, rub some of its blood on the lobe of the right ear of the one seeking cleansing, on the thumb of his right hand, and on the big toe of his right foot.

[Leviticus 14:13a, 14]

26 Then the priest shall pour some of the oil on his left palm, **27** and spatter with his right hand the oil from his left palm 7 times before Jehovah.

[Leviticus 14:16]

28 The priest shall rub the oil that is in his palm on the lobe of the right ear of the one seeking cleansing, on the thumb of his right hand and on the big toe of his right foot, over the blood of the guilt offering.

[Leviticus 14:17]

29 And the priest shall rub the remaining oil in his palm on the head of the one seeking cleansing by which to take away his sins before Jehovah.

[Leviticus 14:18]

30 Then he shall present the 2 turtle doves or 2 the young pigeons, whichever he can afford, **31** the one as a sin offering and the other as a burnt offering, along with the grain offering. Thus the priest has taken the sin of the one seeking cleansing before Jehovah.

[Leviticus 12:7-8]

32 This, then, is the procedure for one who is cured of infectious skin disease but cannot afford the cost of cleansing."

33 Jehovah went on to say to Moses and Aaron:

34 "When you are already in the land of Canaan, which I am giving as your inheritance, and I plagued one of the houses there with virus,

35 the owner of that house shall go and say to the priest, 'There is some kind of virus in my house' ---

36 And the priest shall give an order that the house be vacated before he comes to examine the house, otherwise he may declare everything that is in the house unclean. Afterwards the priest shall come to examine the house.

37 After he examines the house and finds greenish or reddish indentations on its walls, which appear to be deeper than the surface of the wall, **38** the priest shall leave the house through its door and quarantine the house 7 days.

39 On the 7th day the priest shall come back and take a look.

If the virus has spread on the walls of the house, **40** then the priest shall give orders that the bricks, in which the virus is, be removed and dumped to a *landfill* outside the city.

41 Then he will have the whole interior of the house be scraped, and the scraped-off plaster be dumped to a *landfill* outside the city.

42 They shall replace the old bricks with new bricks, and the scraped-off plaster with new plaster.

43 But if the virus comes back and breaks out in the house after the bricks have been removed and the plaster have been replaced, **44** the priest must come back and take a look. If the virus has spread in the house, it is persistent virus; the house is unclean.

[Leviticus 14:41a, 42]

45 He must have the house demolished and have its bricks, timbers, and plasters be dumped to a *landfill* outside the city.

[Leviticus 14:14b]

46 Whoever enters that house while it is in quarantine shall be unclean till evening.

47 And whoever sleeps or eats in that house shall wash his clothes.

48 But if the priest comes back and examines the house, and the virus has not spread after plastering the house, he should pronounce the house clean because the virus has gone away.

49 And to cleanse the house from sin, the priest shall bring 2 birds, cedar wood, red yarn, and hyssop.

[Leviticus 14:4a]

50 He shall drown the one bird in a clay pot by running water.

[Leviticus 14:5]

51 He shall dip the live bird, the cedar wood, the hyssop, and the red yarn in the blood of the bird that was drowned by running water, and then spatter the blood toward the house 7 times.

[Leviticus 14:6-7]

52 Thus he has taken away the sins from the house by the blood of the bird that was drowned by running water, along with the live bird, cedar wood, hyssop, and red yarn.

53 Then he shall release the live bird into the open field outside the city. And after he has taken away the sins from the house, it shall be clean.

[Leviticus 14:7; 17:11; Hebrews 9:19-22]

54 These, then, are the regulations for any infectious skin disease, for the disease causing hair loss, **55** for infected garment or house, **56** for skin rash, scab, and blotchy skin, **57** and to distinguish the clean from the unclean.

[Leviticus 10:10]

CHAPTER 15

1 Jehovah went on to say to Moses and Aaron:

2 "Say to the Israelites, 'When fluid leaks from the penis of a man, such discharge is unclean.

3 And the discharge, whether continuous or blocked, makes him unclean.

4 Any bed or any object on which the man (who has a continuous discharge) lies on or sits shall be unclean.

5 Whoever touches his bed shall wash his clothes and take a bath, and he shall be unclean till evening.

6 Whoever sits on the object on which the man (who has a continuous discharge) has sat shall wash his clothes and take a bath, and he shall be unclean till evening.

7 Whoever touches the man (who has a continuous discharge) shall wash his clothes and take a bath, and he shall be unclean till evening.

8 If the man (who has a continuous discharge) spat on someone who is clean, that one should wash his clothes and take a bath, and he shall be unclean till evening.

9 Any saddle on which the man (who has a continuous discharge) rides shall be unclean.

10 And anyone who touches anything that gets under him shall be unclean till evening. And he who picks it up shall wash his clothes and take a bath, and he shall be unclean till evening.

11 Whoever has been touched by the man (who has a continuous discharge), whose hands have not been washed with water, shall wash his clothes and take a bath, and he shall be unclean till evening.

12 Any clay pot that has been touched by the man (who has a continuous discharge) shall be smashed, and any wooden vessel shall be rinsed with water.

13 If the man is cured of his continuous discharge, it would take 7 days for him to be cleansed from his discharge. Then he shall wash his clothes and take a bath in running water, and he shall be clean.

14 On the 8th day he shall bring 2 turtle doves or 2 young pigeons and hand them to the priest at the entrance of the tabernacle before Jehovah.

15 And the priest shall present them, the one as a sin offering and the other as a burnt offering. Thus the priest has cleansed him from his discharge before Jehovah.

16 When a man releases semen, he shall take a bath and be unclean till evening.

17 Any garment and any leather on which his semen gets shall be washed with water and be unclean till evening.

18 The man and the woman who have sexual intercourse shall take a bath and be unclean till evening.

19 A woman who has a discharge of blood shall be unclean 7 days, as when she is on her period. And whoever touches her shall be unclean till evening.

20 Anything on which she lies or sits while she has a discharge of blood shall be unclean.

21 And whoever touches her bed shall wash his clothes and take a bath, and be unclean till evening.

22 Anyone who touches anything she has sat on shall wash his clothes and take a bath, and be unclean till evening.

23 And whatever object that is on the bed when she sits on it shall be unclean till evening.

24 If a man sleeps with her and her blood gets on him, he would be unclean 7 days, and any bed he lies on shall be unclean.

25 Now if a woman's menstrual period is longer than usual, or if she has a flow of blood beyond the normal period, she should be as unclean as when she is on her period as long as she has the flow of blood.

26 Any bed she has lain on, or any object she has sat on, while she has a flow of blood, shall be as unclean as during her period.

27 Whoever touches them shall be unclean, and he/she shall wash his clothes and take a bath, and be unclean till evening.

28 If she is cured of her flow of blood, it would take 7 days for her to be cleansed, and then she shall be clean.

29 And on the 8th day she shall bring 2 turtle doves or 2 young pigeons to the priest at the entrance of the tabernacle.

[Leviticus 15:14; Numbers 6:10; Luke 2:24]

30 The priest shall present the one as a sin offering and the other as a burnt offering. Thus the priest shall cleanse her from her unclean flow of blood before Jehovah.

[Leviticus 15:15; Numbers 6:11]

31 Keep the Israelites away from anything that can make them unclean, that they may not die in their uncleanness, for defiling My tabernacle which is in their midst.

32 These, then, are the regulations for a man who has a continuous discharge, for a man who releases semen and thus become unclean by it, **33** for a woman undergoing menstruation, for anyone who has a discharge of blood, male or female, and for a man who sleeps with an unclean woman."

CHAPTER 16

1 Now after the death of the two sons of Aaron for burning incense without Jehovah authorizing them,

2 Jehovah said to Moses: "Tell your brother Aaron not to enter at any time the Most Holy Place, that is, beyond the curtain in front of the cover of the Box on which I come down in a cloud, or he shall die.

[Exodus 25:22; 30:6; 40:3; Numbers 7:89; 17:4; Hebrews 6:19-20; 9:3]

3 Before entering the Most Holy Place, Aaron must bring a bull calf as a sin offering, and a male lamb as a burnt offering, to the entrance of the tabernacle.

[Leviticus 16:6, 11, 14, 18, 27]

4 He shall take a bath before wearing the sacred garments. He shall put on the linen shorts and the holy linen robe, and tie the linen sash to him and wrap the linen turban around his head.

[Exodus 28:4, 31; 39:22, 27-29; Leviticus 6:10a; Ezekiel 44:18; Revelation 19:8]

5 Then he shall take from the Israelite community 2 male kid goats as a sin offering and 1 male lamb as a burnt offering.

[Leviticus 16:7]

6 And Aaron shall present the bull calf as a sin offering by which to take away his sins and those of his household.

[Leviticus 16:3, 11, 14, 18, 27]

7 Then he shall present the 2 male kid goats before Jehovah at the entrance of the tabernacle.

[Leviticus 16:5]

8 Aaron shall cast lots on the 2 goats, one lot 'for Jehovah', and the other lot 'for Azazel'.

9 After that Aaron shall present the goat, on which the lot 'for Jehovah' fell, as a sin offering.

[Leviticus 16:8, 15, 18]

10 But the goat on which the lot 'for Azazel' fell shall be presented alive before Jehovah by which to take away sins, for it shall be sent away to the wilderness as a *scapegoat*.

[Leviticus 16:8, 22]

11 Then Aaron shall slaughter the bull calf which he has presented as a sin offering by which to take away his sins and those of his household.

[Leviticus 16:3, 6, 14, 18, 27]

12 Then he shall take a fire holder full of burning coals from the offering stand *(for burnt offerings)* before Jehovah, and 2

handfuls of powdered scented incense, and bring them *beyond* the curtain *(the Most Holy Place)*.

13 He shall put the incense on the burning coals before Jehovah and let the smoke spread over the cover of the Box, where the Commandments are, that he may not die.

[Leviticus 10:1]

14 And he shall spatter with his fingers the blood of the calf's blood 7 times on the east side of the cover, and then spatter with his fingers some of the blood 7 times towards the cover.

[Leviticus 16:3, 6, 11, 18, 27]

15 Then he shall slaughter the goat as a sin offering for the people, bring its blood beyond the curtain, and do with its blood the same as what he did with the calf's blood, that is, spatter it on the east side of the cover and towards the cover.

[Leviticus 16:5, 7, 18, 27]

16 Thus he has taken away from the Most Holy Place all the uncleanness of the Israelites and all their rebellious acts. And he shall do the same for the Holy Place which is in the midst of their uncleanness.

[Leviticus 17:11; Ezekiel 43:20; Hebrews 9:21-22]

17 No one else shall be in the tabernacle from the time he enters to take away the sins from the Holy Place to the time he comes out, that is, to take away his sins, the sins of his household, and the sins of the whole Israelite community.

18 Then he shall go out to the offering stand *(for burnt offerings)* that is before Jehovah to take away the sins from it, by rubbing some of the calf's blood and some of the goat's blood on all its horns.

[Leviticus 16:3, 5-7, 11, 14-15, 27]

19 Then he shall spatter with his fingers the remaining blood all over it 7 times, thus cleansing it and sanctifying it from all the uncleanness of the Israelites.

[Leviticus 17:11; Ezekiel 43:20; Hebrews 9:21-22]

20 After he has taken away the sins from the Most Holy Place, from the Holy Place, and from the offering stand, he shall present the live goat.

[Leviticus 16:33]

21 And Aaron shall lay his hands on the head of the live goat and confess over it all the sins and rebellious acts of the Israelites. In this way he transferred their sins on the goat, which shall be sent away into the wilderness by a man assigned to do it.

[Leviticus 16:8, 10, 22, 26]

22 When the goat is sent away to the wilderness, it brings all their sins to an empty land.

[Leviticus 16:8, 10, 21, 26]

23 Then Aaron shall enter the Holy Place, take off the linen garments that he was wearing when he entered the Most Holy Place, and leave them there.

[Ezekiel 42:14; 44:19]

24 Then he shall take a bath in a clean place, put on his garments, and come out to present his burnt offering and the people's offering by which to take away his sins and those of the people.

[Leviticus 1:4b, 4:20, 31b, 35b; 5:6b, 10b, 13b; 6:6-7, 9:7-8; 12:6--8; 14:30-31; 15:14-15, 29-30; 16:6, 11, 27; 17:11; 19:22; Matthew 26:28; Hebrews 9:13-14]

25 He shall roast all the fat of the sin offering on the offering stand.

[Genesis 4:4; Leviticus 4:24-26; 16:25]

26 And the man who sent away the goat as 'Scapegoat' shall wash his clothes and take a bath. Afterwards he may enter the camp.

[Leviticus 16:8, 10, 21-22]

27 However, he shall have the calf and the goat as sin offerings (which blood were brought to the Most Holy Place) be brought outside the camp, where their skin, flesh, and intestines shall be burned.

[Leviticus 16:3, 5-7, 11, 14-15, 18]

28 And he who burned them shall wash his clothes and take a bath. Afterwards he may enter the camp.

29 This is a lasting ordinance for all of you: On the 10th day of the 7th month, you must fast and do no work, whether you are a citizen or a settler.

[Leviticus 23:27-31; Numbers 29:7; Psalms 35:13b]

30 On such day your sins are to be taken away so you will be pronounced clean. All your sins shall be pardoned before Jehovah.

31 This is a lasting ordinance: Observe sabbath as a day of rest, on which you must fast. **[Leviticus 23:32]**

32 The priest who is anointed and ordained to succeed his father as *high* priest shall put on the sacred linen garments to take sins away.

[Exodus 28:5-6, 8, 15, 39, 42; 39:2-3, 5, 8, 27-29]

33 He shall take away the sins from the Most Holy Place, from the Holy Place, and from the offering stand, More so, he shall take away the sins of the priests and the sins of the whole community.

34 This is a lasting ordinance for you: All the sins of the Israelites shall be taken away every year." **[Hebrews 9:25]**

And he (Aaron) did so, just as Jehovah had told through Moses.

CHAPTER 17

1 Jehovah went on to say to Moses:

2 "Say to Aaron, to his sons, and to all the Israelites, 'Jehovah has given the following commands:

3 Anyone of the house of Israel who slaughters a bull calf or a male lamb or a kid goat inside or outside the camp, **4** and does not bring it to the entrance of the tabernacle and there offer it as a sacrifice to Jehovah, he shall be charged with bloodshed. And the man who has shed blood shall be purged from his people.

[Leviticus 17:9]

5 This is so that the Israelites may bring their offerings to Jehovah at the entrance of the tabernacle, instead of offering them in the open field. They must bring them to the priest who shall offer them as fellowship sacrifices to Jehovah.

[Exodus 29:42]

6 And the priest shall spatter the blood on the offering stand that is before Jehovah at the entrance of the tabernacle, and *on it* he shall roast all the fat for a sweet savor to Jehovah.

7 Thus they would no longer offer their sacrifices to demons, with whom they connive. This is a lasting ordinance for all of you throughout your generations.'

[Deuteronomy 32:17a; 2 Chronicles 11:15; 1 Corinthians 10:20]

8 And say to them, 'Anyone of the house of Israel, or any settler living in your midst, who offers a burnt offering or a fellowship sacrifice 9 and does not bring it to the entrance of the tabernacle and there offer it to Jehovah, shall be purged from his people.

[Leviticus 17:4]

10 I will surely turn My attention against anyone of the house of Israel, or any settler living in your midst, who eats blood of any kind, and purge that person from his people.

[Leviticus 7:27; 17:14c]

11 It's because the life of the flesh is in the blood. That is why I have it spattered on the offering stand by which to take away your sins. Blood can take away sin because of the life in it.

[Exodus 24:8; Matthew 26:28; Hebrews 9:12-22]

12 Hence I have told the Israelites, 'No one among you, and no settler living in your midst, may eat blood.'

[Genesis 9:4; Leviticus 3:17; 7:26; 19:26a; Deuteronomy 12:16a, 23-25; 15:23a; Acts 15:20, 29; 21:25]

13 When a citizen of Israel, or a settler living in your midst, catches a wild animal or a bird that may be eaten, he must drain it of all its blood and cover the blood with dust.

[Leviticus 1:15b; 17:13; Deuteronomy 12:16b, 24b; 15:23b]

14 That is why I have told the Israelites, 'You must not eat the blood of any kind of flesh, because the life of every flesh is in its blood. Whoever eats blood shall be purged.'

[Leviticus 7:27; 17:10]

15 The person who eats the flesh of an animal found dead or mangled by a wild beast *(as they were not drained of their blood)*, whether he is a citizen or a settler, shall wash his clothes and take a bath, and be unclean till evening, and then he shall be clean.

[Exodus 22:31b; Leviticus 11:40; 22:8]

16 He who will not wash his clothes and not take a bath shall be held liable."

CHAPTER 18

1 Jehovah went on to say to Moses:

2 "Say to the Israelites, 'I am Jehovah your God.

3 Do not imitate the way of Egypt, where you once lived, and the way of Canaan, where I am bringing you. And do not follow their laws.

[Leviticus 18:30]

4 It's My commandments you should obey and it's My laws you should follow. I am Jehovah your God.

[Leviticus 18:26; 19:37; 20:8, 22; 22;31; Deuteronomy 4:5-6; Ecclesiastes 12:13; Ezekiel 20:19]

5 For if a man follows My commandments and My laws, he would live by all means. I am Jehovah.

[Nehemiah 9:29b; Psalms 119:93; Proverbs 4:4; 7:2; Ezekiel 18:9; 20:11; Matthew 19:17; Luke 10:27-28; Romans 10:5; Galatians 3:12]

6 Anyone of you must not go ahead with laying bare the nakedness of any of your close relatives. I am Jehovah.

7 Do not lay bare the nakedness of your mother; it's your father's nakedness.

8 Do not lay bare the nakedness of your stepmother; it's your father's nakedness.

[Leviticus 20:11; Deuteronomy 22:30; 27:20]

9 Do not lay bare the nakedness of your half-sister, whether the daughter of your father or the daughter of your mother, and whether or not you were born in the same house; it's your *parent's* nakedness.

[Leviticus 20:17; Deuteronomy 27:22]

10 Do not lay bare the nakedness of your granddaughter, whether she is the daughter of your son or the daughter of your daughter; it's your nakedness.

11 Do not lay bare the nakedness of your stepmother's daughter, the daughter of your father, she is your half-sister.

12 Do not lay bare the nakedness of your father's sister, she is your aunt.

13 Do not lay bare the nakedness of your mother's sister, she is your aunt.

[Leviticus 20:19]

14 Do not lay bare the nakedness of your uncle's wife, she is your aunt in-law.

[Leviticus 20:20]

15 Do not lay bare the nakedness of your son's wife, she is your daughter-in-law.

[Leviticus 20:12]

16 Do not lay bare the nakedness of your brother's wife; it's your brother's nakedness.

[Leviticus 20:21]

17 Do not lay bare the nakedness of a mother and her daughter, nor shall you lay bare the nakedness of a mother and her granddaughter, whether the daughter of her son or the daughter of her daughter. They are close relatives; it's depravity.

[Leviticus 20:14; Deuteronomy 27:23]

18 Do not lay bare the nakedness of your wife's sister, thus making them rivals.

19 Do not go ahead with laying bare the nakedness of a woman when she is on her period.

[Leviticus 15:24; 20:18]

20 Do not release your semen to someone else's wife and thus become unclean by it.

21 Do not let any of your children be sacrificed to Molech and thus profane the name of your God. I am Jehovah.

[Leviticus 20:2-5]

22 Do not have sex with a man the same way you do with a woman; it's repulsive.

[Leviticus 20:13; Romans 1:27]

23 Do not release your semen to any animal and thus become unclean by it, nor must a woman mate with an animal; it's perversion.

[Exodus 22:19; Leviticus 20:15-16; Deuteronomy 27:21]

24 Do not make yourselves unclean by any of these practices, for by such practices the nations whom I am driving out from before you have made themselves unclean.

[Deuteronomy 18:12]

25 And because the land is unclean, I will bring punishment on it for its sins, and the land will vomit out its inhabitants.

26 You shall keep My commandments and My laws.

[Leviticus 18:4; 19:37; 20:8, 22; 22:31; Deuteronomy 4:5-6; Ecclesiastes 12:13; Ezekiel 20:19]

Do not do any of such abominable practices, whether you are a citizen or a settler.

27 The land is unclean because the people of the land prior to you have done all these abominable practices.

28 And just as it had vomited out the nations prior to you, so it shall vomit you out.

[Leviticus 20:22b]

29 The person who does any of these abominable practices shall be purged from his people.

30 You shall perform Your obligatory duty to Me. Do not do any of the abominable practices that have been practiced before you, for by doing so you will make yourselves unclean. I am Jehovah your God.'"

[Leviticus 18:3]

CHAPTER 19

1 Jehovah went on to say to Moses:

2 "Say to the whole Israelite community, 'Keep yourselves clean, because I, Jehovah your God, am clean.

[Exodus 22:31a; Leviticus 11:44-45; 20:7, 26; Numbers 15:40; 1 Peter 1:15-16]

3 Respect your parents and observe My sabbaths. I am Jehovah your God.

[Exodus 20:12; 31:13a, 16; Leviticus 19:30a; 26:2a; Deuteronomy 5:15b-16; Proverbs 1:8; 4:1; 19:26; Matthew 15:4; 19:19a; Mark 7:10; 10:19; Luke 18:20; Ephesians 6:1-3; Colossians 3:20]

4 Do not turn to worthless gods and do not worship carved images. I am Jehovah your God.

[Exodus 20:4; 34:17; Leviticus 26:1; Deuteronomy 4:15-19, 23b, 25; 5:8; 9:12, 16; 16:21-22; 27:15; 1 Kings 14:9; 2 Kings 17:12, 41; 21:11b; Psalms 78:58; 97:7; 106:19-20, 36; 115:4-8; 135:15-18; Isaiah 2:8-9; 40:18-20, 25; 41:29; 42:8, 17; 44:9-20; 45:20b; 46:5-7; Jeremiah 2:11, 27-28; 8:19b; 10:3-5, 14-15; 14:22; 51:17-18; Ezekiel 22:4b; 44:10, 12; Hosea 8:4c-6b; 13:2; Micah 1:7a; 5:13-14; Nahum 1:14; Habakkuk 2:18-19; Acts 17:29-30; Revelation 9:20]

5 When you offer a fellowship sacrifice to Jehovah, offer it in such a way that it will be credited to you.

6 It shall be eaten on the day you offer it and on the next day, but what remains till the 3rd day shall be burned up.

[Exodus 12:10; 29:34; Leviticus 7:17; 8:32]

7 If ever it is eaten on the 3rd day, it would not be accepted; it is spoiled.

[Leviticus 7:18]

8 And the person who eats it shall be held liable for profaning a holy thing of Jehovah. He must be purged from his people.

9 When you reap the harvest of your land, do not reap to the very edges of your field and do not collect the bits and pieces of your harvest.

[Leviticus 23:22]

10 Neither must you strip your vineyard bare nor pick up the grapes that have fallen. Leave them for the needy and for the settlers. I am Jehovah your God.

11 Do not steal, deceive, and cheat.

[Exodus 20:15; Leviticus 19:13a; 25:14, 17; Deuteronomy 5:19; Matthew 19:18; Mark 10:19; Luke 18:20; Romans 13:9; Ephesians 4:28]

12 Do not swear to a lie by My name and thus profane the name of your God. I am Jehovah.

[Exodus 20:7; Leviticus 22:32; Deuteronomy 5:11]

13 Do not defraud one another and do not extort. Do not hold back the wages of a hired worker even for a day.

[Leviticus 19:11; Deuteronomy 24:15; Malachi 3:5; James 5:4]

14 Do not curse the deaf and do not put an obstacle before the blind. Be in fear of your God. I am Jehovah.

[Deuteronomy 27:18]

15 Do not be unfair. Do not show bias towards the lowly, and do not favor the rich. Treat every human being equally.

[Exodus 23:3; Deuteronomy 1:17; Job 32:21a; Proverbs 18:5; 24:23; 28:21a; James 2:3-4, 9]

16 Do not gad about gossiping among your people. Do not bear false witness to a crime punishable by death. I am Jehovah.

[Exodus 20:16; 23:1-2, 7; Psalms 15:1-3; Proverbs 6:17]

17 Do not harbor a grudge against your brother. By all means rebuke your friend if you do not want to be part of his sin.

[Proverbs 24:25; 27:5; Ezekiel 3:21; Matthew 18:15; Luke 17:3]
18 Do not avenge yourself nor harbor a grudge against your kinsmen. Love others as yourself. I am Jehovah.

[Matthew 19:19b; 22:39; Mark 12:31a; Luke 10:27b; Romans 12:19; 13:9b; Galatians 5:14; James 2:8]

19 Keep these regulations of Mine:

Do not crossbreed 2 different kinds of farm animals.
Do no sow your field with 2 different kinds of seed.
Do not wear a garment made of 2 different fabrics.

[Deuteronomy 22:9-11]

20 When a man have sex with a female slave who is engaged to another man, but she has not been bought back nor has been set free, there should be penalty, but not with death, because she is not a freewoman.

21 And he shall bring a male sheep as his guilt offering to Jehovah at the entrance of the tabernacle.

[Leviticus 1:10; 17:3-4]

22 By the male sheep as a guilt offering the priest shall take away his sin before Jehovah, for the crime he has committed, and he shall be pardoned.

[Leviticus 6:6-7; 19:21-22]

23 When you are already in the land and have planted a fruit tree, regard its fruit as unclean 'foreskin'; it should not be eaten. For 3 years consider the fruit tree as 'uncircumcised'.

24 But in the 4th year all its fruit shall be clean, a cause for celebration to Jehovah.

25 And in the 5th year you may eat its fruit, and it will increase its yield for you. I am Jehovah your God.

26 Eat nothing along with blood.

[Genesis 9:4; Leviticus 3:17; 7:26-27; 17:10-14; 19:26a; Deuteronomy 12:16, 23-25; 15:23; Acts 15:20, 29; 21:25]

Do not read *horoscope*, and do not practice magic.

[Deuteronomy 18:10]

27 Do not shave your sideburn, and do not trim your beard.

[Leviticus 21:5b]

28 Do not make cuts in your body for a dead person, and do not tattoo your bodies. I am Jehovah.

[Leviticus 21:5c; Deuteronomy 14:1; 1 Kings 18:28]

29 Do not let your daughter be a harlot, lest the land fall into harlotry and be filled with immorality.

[Deuteronomy 23:17]

30 Observe My Sabbaths and revere My tabernacle. I am Jehovah.

[Exodus 16:23a; 31:13a, 16; Leviticus 19:3b; 26:2; Deuteronomy 5:15b; Ezekiel 44:24d]

31 Do not turn to spirit mediums and do not consult fortune tellers and thus become unclean by them. I am Jehovah your God.

[Leviticus 20:6; Deuteronomy 18:11-12]

32 Rise before the gray-headed and be considerate of the elderly. Be in fear of your God. I am Jehovah.

33 Do not oppress a settler living in your land.

[Exodus 22:21; 23:9]

34 Treat the settler living among you like a citizen of yours. Love him as yourself, for you were once settlers in Egypt. I am Jehovah your God.

[Leviticus 19:18b; Deuteronomy 10:19; Matthew 19:19b; 22:39; Mark 12:31a; Luke 10:27b; Romans 13:9b; Galatians 5:14; James 2:8]

35 Do not cheat when counting, measuring, and weighing, solid or liquid.

[Deuteronomy 25:16]

36 Have accurate scales and accurate weights for exact volume of ephah *(solid)* and exact volume of hin *(liquid)*. I am Jehovah your God who took you out of Egypt.

[Deuteronomy 25:13-15; Proverbs 11:1; 16:11; 20:10; Ezekiel 45:10]

37 Follow all My commandments and My laws and put them into practice. I am Jehovah.'"

[Leviticus 18:4, 26; 20:8, 22; 22:31; Deuteronomy 4:5-6; Ecclesiastes 12:13; Ezekiel 20:19]

CHAPTER 20

1 Jehovah went on to say to Moses:

2 "Say to the Israelites, 'Any Israelite, and any settler living in Israel, who sacrifices any of his children to Molech shall be put to death without fail. The people of the land shall stone him to death.

[Leviticus 18:21a]

3 As for Me, I will turn My attention against that man and purge him from his people for sacrificing any of his children to Molech, thereby defiling My tabernacle and thus profane My holy name.

[Leviticus 18:21b]

4 If the people of the land deliberately close their eyes when the man sacrifices any of his children to Molech and not put him to death, **5** I, for My part, would turn My attention against that man and his family and purge him, along with all who connived with him and who connived with Molech.

6 I will turn My attention against the person who consults spirit mediums and fortune tellers and thus connive with them, and purge him from his people.

[Leviticus 19:31; 1 Chronicles 10:13]

7 Cleanse yourselves and keep yourselves clean because I, Jehovah your God, am sanctifying you.

[Exodus 22:31a; Leviticus 11:44-45; 19:2; 20:26; 21:8; Numbers 15:40; 1 Peter 1:15-16]

8 Follow My laws and put them into practice. I, Jehovah your God, am sanctifying you.

[Leviticus 18:4, 26; 19:37; 20:22; 22:31; Deuteronomy 4:5-6; Ecclesiastes 12:13; Ezekiel 20:19]

9 Whoever curses his father or his mother shall be put to death without fail. It's his parents whom he cursed; he is responsible for his own death.

[Exodus 21:17; Proverbs 20:20; 30:17; Matthew 15:4; Mark 7:10]

10 A man who have sex with someone else's wife commits adultery. The adulterer, as well as the adulteress, shall be put to death without fail.

[Deuteronomy 22:22]

11 A man who sleeps with his stepmother lays bare the nakedness of his father. Both of them *(he and his stepmother)* shall be put to death without fail; they are responsible for their own death.

[Leviticus 18:8; Deuteronomy 22:30; 27:20]

12 When a man sleeps with his daughter-in-law, it is incest. Both of them shall be put to death without fail; they are responsible for their own death.

[Leviticus 18:15]

13 When a man sleeps with a man, just like sleeping with a woman, both of them do a repulsive thing. They shall be put to death without fail; they are responsible for their own death.

[Leviticus 18:22; Romans 1:27]

14 When a man have sex with a mother and her daughter, it is depravity. All of them must be burned to death so that depravity will not go on in your midst.

[Leviticus 18:17; Deuteronomy 27:23]

15 When a man releases his semen to an animal, he shall be put to death without fail, and the animal you shall kill.

[Exodus 22:19; Deuteronomy 27:21]

16 When a woman mates with an animal, the woman shall be put to death without fail, and the animal you shall kill.

[Exodus 22:19]

They are responsible for their own death.

17 When a man lays bare the nakedness of his half-sister, whether the daughter of his father or the daughter of his mother, it is incest. They shall be purged from their people. He shall be held liable for laying bare the nakedness of his sister.

[Leviticus 18:9; Deuteronomy 27:22]

18 When a man sleeps with a woman when she is on her period, he lays bare her nakedness and exposes her source of blood. Both of them shall be purged from their people.

[Leviticus 15:24; 18:19]

19 Do not lay bare the nakedness of your mother's sister or of your father's sister, it's the nakedness of your aunt. Both of you *(you and your aunt)* shall be held liable.

[Leviticus 18:12-13]

20 When a man sleeps with his uncle's wife, he lays bare the nakedness of his uncle. Both of them *(he and his uncle's wife)* shall be held liable for their sin; they shall die childless.

[Leviticus 18:14]

21 When a man sleeps with his brother's wife, he lays bare the nakedness of his brother. It is repugnant; they shall die childless.

[Leviticus 18:16]

22 Follow all My commandments and My laws and put them into practice, that the land, to where I'm bringing you to live in, may not vomit you out.

[Leviticus 18:4, 26-28; 19:37; 20:8; 22:31; Deuteronomy 4:5-6; Ecclesiastes 12:13; Ezekiel 20:19]

23 Do not follow the laws of the nations whom I'm driving away from before you. I hate them because they are doing all these things.

[Leviticus 18:3; Deuteronomy 7:1; 9:5]

24 Thus I told you, 'Your part is to take possession of their land, while My part is to give it to you so you can possess it, a land overflowing with milk and honey. I, Jehovah your God, set you apart from the peoples.'

[Exodus 3:8, 17b; Leviticus 20:26b; Deuteronomy 31:20a; Jeremiah 11:5; 32:22; Ezekiel 20:6, 15]

25 Thus you can distinguish clean animal from unclean one, and clean bird from unclean one. Do not defile yourselves by an animal or by a bird or by any creature that creeps on the ground, which I have separated from you by pronouncing them unclean.

[Leviticus 10:10; 11:47]

26 Keep yourselves clean in My eyes, because I, Jehovah, am clean. I am setting you apart from the peoples that you may be Mine.

[Exodus 22:31a; Leviticus 11:44-45; 19:2; 20:7, 24b; Numbers 15:40; 1 Peter 1:15-16]

27 A spirit medium or a fortune-teller, male or female, shall be put to death without fail. They should be stoned to death; they are responsible for their own death.'"

[Exodus 22:18]

CHAPTER 21

1 Jehovah went on to say to Moses: "Say to Aaron's sons the priests, 'No one may defile himself for a dead person among his people.

[Numbers 19:11]

2 But for his immediate family such as his father and his mother, for his son and for his daughter, and for his brother 3 and for his sister who was a virgin close to him, he may defile himself.

[Ezekiel 44:25]

4 But he may not defile himself for a (dead) married woman among his people and thus defile himself.

5 They must not shave their head bald, they must not trim their beard, and they must not make any cuts in their body.

[Leviticus 19:27-28a; Deuteronomy 14:1]

6 They must keep themselves clean in the eyes of their God and not profane the name of their God. They should keep themselves clean because they are the ones who present roasted offerings to Jehovah, the food of their God.

[Leviticus 1:9, 13, 17; 2:2, 9, 16; 3:5, 16; 4:31a; 6:14-15, 20-21]

7 They may not marry a prostitute or a violated woman or a divorced woman, for they are to be clean in the eyes of their God.

[Leviticus 21:14; Ezekiel 44:22]

8 You shall sanctify them because they are the ones who present the food of your God. Regard them as holy, because I, Jehovah, who sanctifies you is holy

9 If a priest's daughter is promiscuous, it's her father whom she is defiling. She should be burned *to death*.

10 The high priest among the brothers, on whose head the anointing oil is poured and who is ordained to wear the *(sacred)* garments, must not leave his hair uncombed and must not rend his clothes.

[Leviticus 10:6]

11 He must not go near to a dead person. Even for his dead father or for his dead mother he may not defile himself.

[Numbers 19:11]

12 More so, he may not leave the tabernacle and thus defile it, because he wears the label of holiness and the anointing oil of his God is poured on him. I am Jehovah.

[Leviticus 10:7]

13 He may only marry a virgin.

14 He may not marry a widow or a divorced woman or a violated woman or a prostitute, but only a virgin from among his people.

[Leviticus 21:7; Ezekiel 44:22]

15 He must not degrade his children before his people, for I, Jehovah, am sanctifying him.'"

16 Jehovah went on to say to Moses:

17 "Say to Aaron, 'None of their offspring, throughout their generations, who has a physical defect may come and present the food of his God.

[Leviticus 21:21]

18 Whoever has any of the following physical defects may not come:

blind, lame, with slit nose, with one limb too long,

19 a man with crippled foot or hand,

20 a hunchback or a *dwarf* or with eye defect or scabby or with ringworms or with damaged testicles.

[Leviticus 22:24; Deuteronomy 23:1]

21 Anyone of the descendants of Aaron the priest who has a physical defect may not come and present roasted offerings to Jehovah. Because he has a physical defect, he may not come and present the food of his God.

[Leviticus 21:17]

22 However, he may eat the food of his God, from the holy part to the holiest part.

23 But since he has a physical defect, he may not go beyond the curtain *to burn incense* and thus defile My tabernacle, for I, Jehovah, am sanctifying them.'"

24 And Moses spoke thus to Aaron, to his sons, and to all the Israelites.

CHAPTER 22

1 Jehovah went on to say to Moses:

2 "Tell Aaron and his sons to keep themselves separate from the things the Israelites dedicate to Me, and not profane My holy name by the things they dedicate to Me. I am Jehovah.

3 Say to them, 'Anyone of your descendants throughout your generations who goes near the things the Israelites dedicate to Jehovah, while he is unclean, shall be purged from before Me. I am Jehovah.

4 None of Aaron's descendants who has a skin disease or has a continuous discharge may eat of the holy things until he becomes clean, nor he who has touched someone made unclean by a dead body, nor a man who has released semen;

5 nor a man who has touched any swarming insect he is to regard as unclean, or who has touched a man he is to regard as unclean, whatever his uncleanness may be.

[Leviticus 5:2-3; 11:43, 44b; 20:25]

6 The person who touches any such shall be unclean till evening, and may not eat any of the holy things until he has taken a bath.

7 When the sun goes down, he shall be clean, and then he may eat of the holy things, for these are the food for him.

8 He may not eat any animal found dead or mangled by wild beasts and thus become unclean. I am Jehovah.

[Exodus 22:31b; Leviticus 22:8; Deuteronomy 14:21a]

9 They shall perform their obligatory duty to Me, that they may not incur sin and have to die. I, Jehovah, am sanctifying them.

10 No *non-Aaronite* may eat any holy thing. No guest of a priest or a hired worker may eat any holy thing.

[Exodus 12:45; 29:33b]

11 But the person who is bought by a priest with his money, as well as the slaves born in his house, they as such may partake of his food.

12 If the priest's daughter is married to a *non-Aaronite*, she as such may not partake of the holy things.

13 But when the priests' daughter becomes a widow or divorced without a child, she may return to her father's house as when she was young and may partake of her father's food. But no *non-Aaronite* may ever eat of it.

14 If a man eats a holy thing by mistake, he should add 1/5 to the value of the holy thing and give it to the priest.

[Leviticus 5:16a; 6:5b; 27:13, 19; Numbers 5:7]

15 This is so that they may not defile the things the Israelites dedicate to Jehovah, **16** and thereby bear the penalty for eating such holy things. I, Jehovah, am sanctifying them.'"

17 Jehovah went on to say to Moses:

18 "Say to Aaron, to his sons, and to all the Israelites, 'When anyone of the house of Israel, or any settler in Israel, presents a burnt offering to Jehovah, whether a vow offering or a freewill offering, **19** it shall be from the flock, either a lamb or a kid goat, male without defect, and it will be credited to you.

[Leviticus 1:10; 1 Peter 1:18-19]

20 Do not present anything with a physical defect, for it will not be credited to you.

[Deuteronomy 15:21]

21 When a man offers a fellowship sacrifice to Jehovah, whether a vow offering or a freewill offering, it shall be from the herd or from the flock, without defect, For it to be credited to him, there should be no any defect in it.

[Deuteronomy 17:1]

22 No blind or fractured or wounded or with warts or scabs or ringworms must you present to Jehovah, and you may not roast any of them on the offering stand for Jehovah.

[Malachi 1:8, 13-14]

23 You may offer a bull or a sheep with a limb too long or too short as a freewill offering, but not as a vow offering; it will not be accepted.

24 Do not offer *as a sacrifice* to Jehovah one with testicles damaged or crushed or torn or cut off. Do not present such in your land.

25 Do not present any of such from a foreigner as food of your God because there is a defect in them. And because there is a defect in them, they will not be accepted.'"

[Leviticus 22:19-21]

26 Jehovah went on to say to Moses:

27 "A newly born calf or lamb or goat shall stay with its mother 7 days. But from the 8th day onward, it will be accepted as an offering, a roasted offering to Jehovah.

[Exodus 22:30]

28 Do not slaughter a bull or a sheep along with its young on the same day.

29 When you offer a thanksgiving sacrifice to Jehovah, offer it in such a way that it will be credited to you.

30 On that very day it shall be eaten. You must not leave any of it till morning. I am Jehovah.

[Exodus 12:8a, 10a; 23:18; 34:25; Leviticus 7:15; Numbers 9:12a; Deuteronomy 16:4b]

31 Keep My commandments and put them into practice. I am Jehovah.

[Leviticus 18:4, 26; 19:37; 20:8, 22; Deuteronomy 4:5-6; Ecclesiastes 12:13; Ezekiel 20:19]

32 Do not profane My holy name, I must be *given glory* in the midst of the Israelites. I, Jehovah, who sanctifies you, **33** took you out of Egypt to be God to you. I am Jehovah.'"

[Genesis 17:7; Exodus 6:7b; 20:7; 29:45; Leviticus 19:12; 26:12a; Deuteronomy 5:11; 29:13b; 2 Samuel 7:24b; Jeremiah 7:23a; 11:4; 24:7; 30:22; 31:1a, 33b; 32:38; Ezekiel 11:20; 14:11; 34:30a; 36:28; 37:23, 27; Zechariah 8:8; 2 Corinthians 6:16; Hebrews 8:10]

CHAPTER 23

1 Jehovah went on to say to Moses:

2 "Say to the Israelites, 'Declare the annual festivals of Jehovah as holy days.

[Leviticus 23:37; 2 Chronicles 8:13]

3 Six days you may work, but observe sabbath on the 7th day. A day of rest, a holy day; do no work of any kind. Observe sabbath to Jehovah wherever you are.

[Exodus 16:23; 20: 9-10; 23:12; 31:13a, 15-16; 34:21; 35:2-3; Leviticus 19:3b, 30a; 23:3; 26:2a; Deuteronomy 5:13-15]

4 These are the annual festivals of Jehovah you shall proclaim as holy days at their scheduled time and date:

5 The Passover to Jehovah is on the 14th day of the 1st month, between sunset and dusk.

[Exodus 12:6; Numbers 9:2-5; 28:16; Deuteronomy 16:6; Joshua 5:10; 2 Chronicles 30:15a; 35:1; Ezra 6:19; Ezekiel 45:21a]

6 The Feast of Unleavened Bread to Jehovah is on the 15th day of this month, from which you shall eat unleavened bread 7 days.

[Exodus 12:15, 17-18; 13:6-7; 34:18; Numbers 28:17; Deuteronomy 16:3, 16; 2 Chronicles 8:13; 30:21; 35:17; Ezra 6:22a; Ezekiel 45:21b; Luke 22:1; Acts 12:3b; 1 Corinthians 5:8]

7 The 1st day is a holy day; do no hard work of any kind.

[Exodus 12:16a]

8 For 7 days present a roasted offering to Jehovah. The 7th day is also a holy day; do no hard work of any kind.'"

[Exodus 12:16b; 13:6b; Leviticus 23:36; Deuteronomy 16:8b]

9 Jehovah went on to say to Moses:

10 "Say to the Israelites, 'When you are already in the land that I am giving you, and you have harvested its crops, you shall bring a sheaf of the firstfruits of your harvest to the priest.

[Exodus 23:19a; 34:26a; Deuteronomy 26:2; 2 Chronicles 31:5; Nehemiah 10:35; Proverbs 3:9; Ezekiel 44:30]

11 And right after the sabbath day the priest shall wave the sheaf before Jehovah to be credited to you.

12 On the day your sheaf was waved, you shall present a one-year-old male lamb, without defect, as a burnt offering to Jehovah, 13 and 2/10 of an ephah of fine flour sprinkled with oil as its grain offering, as a sweet-savory roasted offering to Jehovah, and ¼ of a hin of wine as its drink offering.

[Genesis 8:21; Exodus 29:18, 25, 41b; Leviticus 1:13b: 8:21; 23:17; Ephesians 5:2b; Philippians 4:18b]

14 You must eat no bread nor grain, roasted or fresh, until the day you have brought your offerings to God. This is a lasting ordinance throughout your generations wherever you are.

15 And from the day you have brought the sheaf as a wave offering, which is the day right after the sabbath, count off 7 sabbaths. They should be exact.

[Deuteronomy 16:9]

16 Then after the 7th sabbath, which is the 50th day, you shall present a new grain offering to Jehovah.

17 From your house you shall take 2 loaves as a wave offering, which should be 2/10 of an ephah of fine flour. They should be made without yeast as ripe firstfruits to Jehovah.

[Leviticus 23:13]

18 To go with the loaves, you shall present 7 one-year-old male lambs, without defect, and 1 bull calf and 2 male sheep as burnt offerings to Jehovah, along with their grain offering and their drink offering, as a sweet-savory roasted offering to Jehovah.

[Leviticus 23:20]

19 More so, present a kid goat as a sin offering, and 2 one-year-old male lambs as a fellowship sacrifice.

20 Along with the 2 male sheep, the priest shall wave the loaves of the firstfruits as a wave offering before Jehovah. And these holy offerings to Jehovah shall belong to the priest.

[Leviticus 23:18]

21 Declare this very day as a holy day; do no hard work of any kind. This is a lasting ordinance throughout your generations wherever you are.

22 When you harvest of crops of your land, do not reap to the very edges of your field and do not collect the bits and pieces of your harvest. Leave them for the needy and the settlers. I am Jehovah your God.

[Leviticus 19:9]

23 Jehovah went on to say to Moses:

24 "Say to the Israelites, 'The 1st day of the 7th month is your day of rest. Sound a trumpet blast to remind everyone that it is a holy day.

[Numbers 10:10; 29:1; Nehemiah 8:2]

25 Do no hard work of any kind, except to present a roasted offering to Jehovah.'"

26 Jehovah went on to say to Moses:

27 "What's more, The Day of Atonement *(the day sins are taken away)* is the 10th *day* of the 7th month. It is your holy day, on which you shall fast and present a roasted offering to Jehovah.

[Leviticus 16:29; 25:9; Acts 27:9]

28 Do no work of any kind on that day, it's the Day of Atonement on which your sins are taken away before Jehovah your God.

[Leviticus 16:30]

29 Every person who would not fast on that day shall be purged from his people.

30 I will destroy whoever among you who does any work on that day.

31 Do no work of any kind. This is a lasting ordinance throughout your generations wherever you are.

[Leviticus 16:31]

32 The Sabbath is your day of rest on which you must fast. Observe sabbath from the evening of the 9th *day* of the month until the following evening.'"

33 Jehovah went on to say to Moses:

34 "Say to the Israelites, 'On the 15th day of the 7th month is the Festival of Booths *(Feast of Ingathering in Exodus 23:16b, while Festival of Tabernacles in John 7:2)* to Jehovah for 7 days.

[Exodus 23:16b; 34:22b; Leviticus 23:39; Deuteronomy 16:13; 2 Chronicles 8:13; Ezra 3:4; Nehemiah 8:14; Zechariah 14:16b]

35 The 1st day is a holy day; do no hard work of any kind.

36 Present a roasted offering to Jehovah 7 days. The 8th day is also a holy day on which you shall present a roasted offering to Jehovah. *Meditate*, do no hard work of any kind.

[Leviticus 23:8; Nehemiah 8:18]

37 These, then, are the annual festivals of Jehovah which you shall declare as holy days, on which you shall present roasted offerings to Jehovah --- burnt offerings with their grain offering and drink offering at their scheduled time and date.

[Leviticus 23:2]

38 You shall present them to Jehovah aside from observing the sabbaths of Jehovah, aside from your offerings, aside from your vow offerings, and aside from your freewill offerings.

[Numbers 29:39]

39 When you have gathered in the crops of the land on the 15th day of the 7th month, celebrate the festival to Jehovah 7 days. The 1st day is a day of rest, as well as the 8th day.

[Leviticus 23:34; Numbers 29:12]

40 On the 1st day, you shall take the fruit of splendid trees, the branches of palm trees, the boughs of leafy trees, and the willows of brooks, and celebrate before Jehovah your God 7 days.

[Nehemiah 8:15; Revelation 7:9]

41 This is a lasting ordinance throughout your generations: Celebrate it as a feast to Jehovah on the 7th month, 7 days a year.

[Nehemiah 8:18]

42 All the citizens of Israel shall dwell in booths 7 days.

43 This is so that your generations may know that I made the Israelites dwell in booths when I took them out of Egypt. I am Jehovah your God.'"

[Nehemiah 8:14]

44 Thus Moses informed the Israelites about the annual festivals of Jehovah.

CHAPTER 24

1 Jehovah went on to say to Moses:

2 "Tell the Israelites to bring you pure virgin olive oil to keep the lamps burning.

[Exodus 27:20]

3 Outside the curtain that screens off the Commandments, in the Holy Place, Aaron shall keep them lit from evening till morning before Jehovah. This is a lasting ordinance throughout your generations.

[Exodus 27:21; 40:4b]]

4 He shall keep in order the lamps of the pure-gold lampstand before Jehovah.

5 Then you shall bake fine flour into 12 round loaves; each round loaf should be 2/10 of an ephah.

6 You shall arrange them in two rows, six layers per row, on the pure-gold coated table before Jehovah.

[Exodus 40:4a, 22]

7 You shall sprinkle pure frankincense on each layer as a token of the roasted offering to Jehovah.

8 This is a lasting covenant with the Israelites: Every Sabbath he shall set them in order before Jehovah.

[1 Chronicles 9:32]

9 And this is a lasting ordinance: It *(the remainder of the fine flour- see Verse 7)*, which is the holiest part of the roasting offering to Jehovah, shall belong to Aaron and his sons, and they shall eat it in a holy place."

[Leviticus 6:16-18; Matthew 12:4; Mark 2:26; Luke 6:4]

10 Now a man, whose father was an Egyptian and whose mother was an Israelite, came to the camp of the Israelites and got into a fight with a pure Israelite man.

11 The man, whose mother was an Israelite woman by the name Shelomith (the daughter of Dibri, of the tribe of Dan) cursed the Name, and so he was brought to Moses.

12 And they detained him until a clear verdict from Jehovah was handed down to them.

[Numbers 15:34]

13 Then Jehovah said to Moses:

14 "Bring the one who cursed outside the camp. And all who heard him shall lay their hands on his head, and the whole community must stone him *to death.*

[Numbers 15:35]

15 Say to the Israelites, 'A man who curses his God shall be held accountable for his sin.

[Exodus 22:28; Numbers 15:30; Deuteronomy 5:11]

16 But he who profanes the name Jehovah shall be put to death without fail. The whole community shall stone him to death without fail. Whether he is a settler or a citizen, he shall be put to death for profaning the Name.

[Jeremiah 29:32b]

17 A man who kills a man shall be put to death without fail.

[Genesis 9:6; Exodus 21:12; Leviticus 24:21b; Numbers 35:30-31]

18 A person who kills a farm animal shall make compensation for it, life for life.

[Exodus 21:23]

19 A man who injures someone, just as he has done, so it shall be done to him:

20 fracture for fracture, eye for eye, tooth for tooth.

[Exodus 21:24; Deuteronomy 19:21; Matthew 5:38a]

The injury he caused in a man shall likewise be done to him.

21 He who kills a farm animal shall make compensation for it, but he who kills a man shall be put to death.

[Exodus 21:12; Leviticus 24:17]

22 The same law applies to both settlers and citizens. I am Jehovah your God.'"

[Exodus 12:49; Leviticus 18:26; Numbers 9:14b; 15:15-16, 29; 19:10b]

23 After that Moses told the Israelites to bring the one who cursed outside the camp and there stone him *to death*. And the Israelites did so, just as Jehovah has told Moses.

[Numbers 15:36]

CHAPTER 25

1 Jehovah spoke to Moses in Mount Sinai:

2 "Say to the Israelites, 'When you are already in the land that I am giving you, let the land have a sabbath rest to Jehovah.

3 Sow your field 6 years and prune your vineyard 6 years, then reap the land's yield.

[Exodus 23:10]

4 But in the 7th year let the land observe sabbath to Jehovah, a year of rest. Do not sow your field and do not prune your vineyard.

[Exodus 23:11a]

5 Neither shall you reap what grows from your spilled kernels nor shall you gather the grapes from your untended vines. Let the land have a year of rest.

6 For even if the land is observing sabbath, still it would produce food for you, for your male slaves and female slaves, for your hired workers and for the settlers in your midst, **7** for your farm animals and for the wild animals that are in your land. All its produce shall serve as your food.

8 You shall count off 7 sabbatical years, 7 times 7, and the total is 49 years.

9 On the 10th day of the 7th month, on the Day of Atonement, you shall sound a loud trumpet blast across your land.

[Leviticus 23:24, 27]

10 You shall sanctify the 50th year and proclaim liberty to all the inhabitants of the land. It will be your Jubilee, when everyone shall return to his property and to his family.

[Leviticus 25:13, 27-28, 41]

11 The 50th year shall be your Jubilee. Neither shall you sow seed nor reap what grows from spilled kernels nor gather the grapes from untended vines.

[Leviticus 25:4]

12 It is Jubilee, regard it as holy. You may eat only what the wild plants yield.

13 In this Year of Jubilee, everyone may return to his property.

[Leviticus 25:10, 27-28, 41]

14 Whether you sell or you buy, do not defraud one other.

[Leviticus 19:11, 13a; 25:17]

15 Buy based on the number of years after the Jubilee, and sell based on the number of crops.

16 And since what is being sold is the number of crops, the more the years, the higher the price; the fewer the years, the lower the price.

[Leviticus 25:50-52]

17 Do not defraud one another, be in fear of your God. I am God.

[Leviticus 19:11, 13a; 25:14]

18 If you keep My commandments and My laws and put them into practice, you would live securely in the land.

[Proverbs 1:33]

19 The land will yield its crops, and you will eat to your fill and live securely.

20 In case you ask, 'What are we going to eat during the 7th year if we would not sow seed nor reap our harvest?'

21 Well, I will command My blessing on you in the 6th year, and it will yield crops for 3 years.

22 Thus you will be eating the old crops till the 9th year, till the coming of the new crops from what you have planted in the 8th year.

[Leviticus 26:10]

23 The land shall not be sold permanently because the land is Mine. You are but strangers and settlers from My standpoint.

[1 Chronicles 29:15a; Psalms 39:12b; 1 Peter 2:11a]

24 Hence there shall be a provision 'the right to buy back' for every piece of your land.

25 If your brother becomes poor and sells away some of his property, a redeemer closely related to him must come and buy back what his brother has sold.

26 If one who has no redeemer becomes rich and can afford to buy it back, **27** he should start to count from the year he has sold it and refund the overpayment to the buyer before he returns to his property.

[Leviticus 27:18]

28 But if he cannot afford to buy back what he has sold, then it shall remain in the possession of the buyer until the Jubilee Year. And in the Jubilee it shall be given back, and he will return to his property.

29 If a man sells a house in a walled city, his right to buy it back expires in a year starting from the date of sale.

30 If a house in the walled city is not bought back before a whole year expires, it would be the permanent property of the buyer and his descendants. It shall not be given back in the Jubilee.

31 However, the houses *in unwalled villages* around them are classified as part of the forest. As such, these can be bought back and be given back in the Jubilee.

32 And the Levites have the perpetual right to buy back the houses in the cities that they owned.

33 If the Levites failed to buy back the house in the city that they own, it should be given back in the Jubilee. It's because the houses in the cities that *they* own are their *permanent* property in the midst of the Israelites.

34 What's more, the pastureland of their city cannot be sold; it is their permanent property.

35 If a brother living near you goes bankrupt and becomes poor, you should provide for him. Keep him alive like a stranger or a settler in your midst.

[Deuteronomy 15:7; Psalms 41:1; Proverbs 19:17; 1 John 3:17-18]

36 You shall not lend him money on interest. Be in fear of your God; let your brother stay alive with you.

[Exodus 22:25; Deuteronomy 23:19; Psalms 15:5]

37 Do not lend him your money on interest and do not give him your food for profit.

[Deuteronomy 23:19b]

38 I, Jehovah your God, took you out of Egypt and gave you the land of Canaan to be God to you.

[Genesis 17:7-8; Exodus 6:7b; 29:45; Leviticus 26:12a; Deuteronomy 29:13; 2 Samuel 7:24; Jeremiah 7:23a; 11:4; 24:7;

30:22; 31:1a, 33; 32:38; Ezekiel 11:20; 14:11; 34:30; 36:28; 37:23, 27; Zechariah 8:8; 2 Corinthians 6:16; Hebrews 8:10]

39 If the brother living near you becomes poor and sells himself to you, you should not make him work like a slave.

[1 Kings 9:22; 2 Chronicles 8:9; Jeremiah 34:9]

40 He may serve you as a hired worker, or like a settler, until the Jubilee Year.

41 But you must set him free, he and his children, so that he can return to his family and to his ancestral property.

[Leviticus 25:10, 13, 27-28]

42 They are My servants whom I took out of Egypt; they must not be sold the way a slave is sold.

[Leviticus 25:55; Nehemiah 1:10]

43 Do not tread them down like a tyrant. Be in fear of your God.

[Leviticus 25:53]

44 You may buy a slave, male or female, from the nations all around you.

45 Or you may buy the children of the settlers living among you, or their relatives who were born in your land; they may become your property.

46 And you can pass them on to your children as permanent property. You may make them your slaves, but not your fellows Israelites. Do not be like tyrants treading down one another.

47 If a stranger or a settler in your midst becomes rich, and your brother living near him becomes poor and sells himself to that stranger or settler in your midst, or to a member of his family,

48 then he has the right to be bought back after he was sold; one of his relatives may buy him back.

[Leviticus 25:53; Nehemiah 5:8a]

49 His uncle or his cousin or any of his immediate family may buy him back. Or he may buy himself back when he becomes rich.

50 He and the buyer shall count how many years more to the year of Jubilee since the he sold himself to him. And his redemption price should be calculated based on the number of years using the wage rate of a contractual worker.

51 But if there are many years more, his redemption price should be calculated based on his sale price.

52 If only a few years remaining until the year of Jubilee, he should compute his redemption price based on the remaining years.

[Leviticus 25:15]

53 In the meantime, *the brother* shall serve *the foreigner* like a contractual worker on annual basis, but he must not tread him down like a tyrant.

[Leviticus 25:43, 47]

54 Now if he cannot buy himself back based on any of these terms, he should go free in the year of Jubilee, he and his children.

[Leviticus 25:49-52]

55 It's because the Israelites are My servants. They are My servants whom I took out of Egypt. I am Jehovah your God.

[Leviticus 25:42]

CHAPTER 26

1 Do not worship worthless gods or carved images. Neither shall you set up an idolatrous post nor erect a monument in your land to which you will bow down. I am Jehovah your God.

[Exodus 20:4; 34:17; Leviticus 19:4; Deuteronomy 4:16-19, 23b, 25; 5:8-9a; 9:12, 16; 16:21-22; 27:15; 1 Kings 9:6-7; 14:9; 2 Kings 17:12, 16, 35, 41; 21:11b; Psalms 78:58; 97:7; 106:19-20, 36; 115:4-8; 135:15-18; Isaiah 2:8-9; 40:18-20, 25; 41:29; 44:9-20; 45:20; 46:5-7; Jeremiah 2:11, 27-28; 8:19b; 10:3-5, 14-15; 51:17-18; Ezekiel 14:6-7; 20:7, 18; 22:4b; 44:10, 12; Hosea 8:4c-6b; 13:2; Micah 1:7a; 5:13-14; Nahum 1:14; Habakkuk 2:18-19; Acts 17:29-30; Revelation 9:20]

2 Observe My Sabbaths and revere My tabernacle. I am Jehovah.

[Exodus 16:23; 31:16; Leviticus 19:3b, 30; Deuteronomy 5:15b; Ezekiel 44:24d; Luke 4:16, 31b; 6:6a; 13:10; Acts 13:44; 18:4]

3 If you follow My commandments and My laws and put them into practice, **4** I would send rain in its season, and the land will yield crops and the fruit trees will bear fruit.

[Deuteronomy 11:14; 28:12; Psalms 85:12; Isaiah 30:23; Ezekiel 34:26-27a; Joel 2:23-24; Zechariah 8:12]

5 Your threshing will last till grape harvest, and your grape harvest till planting time. Thus you can eat to your fill and live securely in your land.

6 I will give peace in the land, and you will lie down with no one making you tremble. I will rid the land of harmful wild beasts, and there will be no war in your land.

[Job 11:19a; Isaiah 35:9; Ezekiel 34:25; Micah 4:4]

7 You will chase your enemies, and they will fall by sword before you.

8 Five of you will chase 100, and 100 of you will chase 10,000, and your enemies will fall by sword before you.

9 I will turn My face to you and make you fruitful. I will multiply you and fulfill My covenant with you.

10 While you are still consuming the old *crops* of the last year, you have to move them out to make room for the new.

[Leviticus 25:22]

11 I will put My tabernacle in your midst, and I will not hate you.

12 I will walk among you and be God to you, and you will be My people.

[Genesis 17:7-8; Exodus 6:7; 29:45; Deuteronomy 29:13; 2 Samuel 7:24; Jeremiah 7:23; 11:4; 24:7; 30:22; 31:1, 33; 32:38; Ezekiel 11:20; 14:11; 34:30; 36:28; 37:23, 27; Hosea 2:23;

Zechariah 8:8; 13:9; Romans 9:25-26; 2 Corinthians 6:16; Hebrews 8:10]

13 I, Jehovah your God, took you out of Egypt so you will no longer be their slaves. I broke the bars of your yoke and made you walk erect.

[Exodus 6:6; 7:4; Deuteronomy 5:15; 7:8; 15:15; Joshua 24:17a; Jeremiah 2:20a; Ezekiel 34:27b; Micah 6:4]

14 But if you will not listen to Me and not follow all these commandments, **15** and if you will reject My laws and abhor My ordinances, so that you do not put them into practice, to the extent that you violate My covenant, **16** I will then punish you, as follows:

I will afflict you with infectious disease and high fever, making your eyes *dry* and your body waste away. You will plant in vain, for your enemies will eat them up.

17 I will turn My face against you, and you will be defeated by your enemies. And those who hate you will tread you down, and you will flee even when no one is chasing you.

[Leviticus 26:36; Deuteronomy 28:25; Proverbs 28:1a]

18 If in spite of all this you will not still listen to me, I would have to discipline you for your sins 7 times over.

[Leviticus 26:21, 24, 28]

19 I will have to break the pride of your power, and make your sky like iron and your soil like bronze.

[Haggai 1:10]

20 You will expend your energy for nothing, for your land will not yield crops and your fruit trees will not bear fruit.

21 If you walk in the opposite direction of Me and refuse to listen to Me, I would have to deal a blow to you for your sins 7 times over.

[Leviticus 26:18, 23-24, 27-28, 40]

22 I will send wild beasts among you, and they will bereave you of your children and will purge your farm animals, leaving you few and your roads deserted.

[Ezekiel 5:17; 14:15]

23 If still you will not submit to My discipline and continue to walk in the opposite direction of Me, **24** then I will walk in the opposite direction of you and strike you for your sins 7 times over.

[Leviticus 26:18, 21, 27-28, 40]

25 I will bring a sword on you to avenge the covenant. When you gather in your cities, I will send a pestilence in your midst, and you will be handed over to your enemy.

[Ezekiel 7:15; Amos 4:10]

26 When I cut off your supply of bread, ten women can bake all your bread in one oven, which they will ration out by weight. You will eat but you will not be satisfied.

[Ezekiel 4:16; 5:16; Hosea 4:10a; Amos 4:6; Micah 6:14a; Haggai 1:6b]

27 If still you will not listen to Me and you walk in the opposite direction of Me, **28** I would have to walk in the opposite direction of you and fiercely punish you for your sins 7 times over.

[Leviticus 27:18, 21, 23-24, 40]

29 You will have to eat the flesh of your sons and of your daughters.

[Deuteronomy 28:53; Jeremiah 19:9; Lamentations 2:20b; 4:10; Ezekiel 5:10a]

30 In disgust I will demolish your mountain shrines, pull down your incense stands, and pile up your corpses on top your lifeless manurelike god icons.

[Ezekiel 6:3-5]

31 I will put your cities to sword, lay your temples in ruins, and not smell your sweet savory offerings.

[Amos 5:21b]

32 As I lay the land desolate, your enemies living there will stare in shock at it.

33 I will scatter you among the nations and will brandish a sword against you, and your land will become desolate and your cities waste.

[Nehemiah 1:8; Jeremiah 9:16; Ezekiel 5:10b, 12; 12:14; 20:23]

34 While you are in the land of your enemies, your land, as it lies desolate, is paying off the sabbaths it missed. And as the land observes sabbath, it is paying off the sabbaths it missed.

[Leviticus 26:43]

35 As long as it lies desolate, it observes sabbath, making up for the sabbaths it missed when you were there.

36 I will traumatize the survivors among you in the land of their enemies. The mere sound of a windblown leaf will send them fleeing, as though fleeing from a sword, and they will fall with no one chasing them.

[Leviticus 26:17]

37 They will stampede as though fleeing from a sword with no one chasing them. As for you, you will not be able stand up against your enemies.

38 You will perish among the nations, and the land of your enemies will eat you up.

39 The survivors among you will rot away in the land of your enemies on account of their sins and their fathers' sins, who likewise rotted away.

40 Then they will confess their sins and their fathers' sins --- that they had been unfaithful to Me for walking in the opposite direction of Me.

[Leviticus 26:21, 23, 27; Daniel 9:4-5]

41 I will walk in the opposite direction of them and have to bring them into the land of their enemies. By then, perhaps their uncircumcised hearts will be humbled and they pay off their sins.

42 Then I will remember My covenant with Jacob, My covenant with Isaac, and My covenant with Abraham, and I will remember the land.

[Exodus 2:24; 6:5; Leviticus 26:45; Psalms 105:42]

43 As long as the land is deserted by them, it is paying off the sabbaths it missed. And as long as it lies desolate without them, they are paying off their sins, for rejecting My commandments and for hating My laws.

[Leviticus 26:32-35]

44 But despite of all this, I will not reject them nor hate them to the point of annihilating them while they are in the land of their enemies. I, Jehovah their God, will not break the covenant I made with them.

[Jeremiah 30:11; Romans 11:2a]

45 In their behalf, I will remember the covenant I made with their forefathers, whom I took out of Egypt before the eyes of the nations to be God to them. I am Jehovah.'"

[Leviticus 11:45; 25:38; 26:42]

46 These, then, are the commandments, the laws, and the ordinances that Jehovah laid on the Israelites in Mount Sinai through Moses.

[Leviticus 27:34]

CHAPTER 27

1 Jehovah went on to say to Moses:

2 "Say to the Israelites, 'When a man makes a special vow to dedicate a person to Jehovah, the value should be set as follows:

3 From 20 to 60 years old ---
the set value for males is 50 silver shekels *(about 10 pounds)* according to the standard sanctuary shekel;

4 the set value for females is 30 shekels *(about 6 pounds)*.

5 From 5 to 20 years old ---
the set value for males is 20 shekels *(about 4 pounds)*, and for females 10 shekels *(about 2 pounds)*.

6 From 1 month to 5 years old ---
the set value for males is 5 silver shekels *(about 1 pound)*, **[Numbers 18:16]**

and for females 3 silver shekels *(about 0.7 pound)*.

7 From 60 years old and above ---
the set value for males is 15 shekels *(about 3 pounds)*, and for females 10 shekels *(about 2 pounds)*.

8 If the vower cannot afford the set value, then he shall present the person to the priest, who shall value him based on what he can afford.

9 If he dedicates an animal to Jehovah, whatever it is that he presents would become holy.

10 He may not substitute nor replace it either with good or with bad. If ever he replaces one for another, both the substituted and the substitute would become holy.

11 If the substitute is an unclean animal that cannot be presented as an offering to Jehovah, he should bring it to the priest.

12 And the priest shall assess it whether it is good or bad. And as the priest values it, so its value shall be.

13 Now if he wants to buy it back, he should add 1/5 to its set value.

[Leviticus 5:16a; 6:5; 22:14; 27:15, 19, 27, 31; Numbers 5:7]

14 When a man dedicates his house to Jehovah, the priest shall assess it whether it is good or bad. And as the priest values it, so its value shall be.

15 If the vower wants to buy his house back, he should add 1/5 to its set value, and he shall retain it.

[Leviticus 5:16a; 6:5b; 22:14; 27:13, 19, 27, 31; Numbers 5:7]

16 When a man dedicates a parcel of his land to Jehovah, its set value shall match the amount of seed planted on it. The set value for a homer of barley seed shall be 50 silver shekels *(about 11 pounds)*.

17 If he dedicates his land in the year of Jubilee, its set value should stand.

18 But if he dedicates his land after the Jubilee, the priest should assess the price for him based on the remaining years until the next Jubilee Year and set a reduced price.

[Leviticus 25:27]

19 If the vower wants to buy his land back, he should add 1/5 to its set value, and he shall retain it.

[Leviticus 5:16a; 6:5b; 22:14; 27:13, 15, 27, 31; Numbers 5:7]

20 If he does not want to buy back his land that was sold to someone else, then it cannot be bought back anymore.

21 The land that is given back in the Jubilee shall become holy, like a land that is reserved for destruction to Jehovah which shall belong to the priest.

22 When one dedicates to Jehovah a land that he has purchased, but which is not part of his inheritance, **23** the priest shall assess the price for him till the Year of Jubilee, and he shall pay the set value on that day. It is holy to Jehovah.

24 In the year of Jubilee, the land shall be given back to the seller, to the original owner.

25 Every value shall be set according to the standard sanctuary shekel, which is 20 gerahs to a shekel.

[Exodus 30:13; Ezekiel 45:12a]

26 However, there is no need to dedicate the firstling of animals to Jehovah. Whether it is a bull or a sheep, it already belongs to Jehovah.

[Exodus 34:19; Numbers 3:13; 8:17]

27 If it is among unclean animals, it should be bought back according to its set value, plus 1/5 to it. If it is not bought back, then it shall be sold at its set value.

[Leviticus 5:16a; 6:5b; 22:14; 27:13, 15, 19, 31; Numbers 5:7]

28 Of all that he has, not a thing that a man has reserved for destruction to Jehovah can be sold or be bought back, whether man or beast, or even the land that he owns. Jehovah regards it as most holy.

[Joshua 6:17a]

29 No person reserved for destruction may be bought back; he should be put to death without fail.

[Joshua 6:21; 8:26; 10:28a, 40; 11:11; 1 Samuel 15:3]

30 And every 10th *produce* of the land, whether of seed or of fruit tree, belongs to Jehovah. Jehovah regards it as holy.

[Deuteronomy 14:22-23; Malachi 3:10; Hebrews 7:5]

31 If a man wants to buy back any of his 10th *produce*, he should add 1/5 to its set value.

[Leviticus 5:16a; 6:5b; 22:14; 27:13, 15, 19, 27; Numbers 5:7]

32 Jehovah regards as holy every 10th head of the herd and of the flock that passes under the shepherd's rod.

[Jeremiah 33:13]

33 Neither shall he examine it nor replace it, whether it is good or bad. But if ever he replaces it, the substituted and the substitute would become holy; it cannot be bought back.'"

34 These, then, are the ordinances that Jehovah had laid on the Israelites in Mount Sinai through Moses.

[Leviticus 26:46]

www.ingramcontent.com/pod-product-compliance
Lightning Source LLC
Chambersburg PA
CBHW031607210526
45464CB00004B/1461